Big I & Me

JOHN M. COFFIN

BIG I & ME

STORIES FROM ITASCA AND BEYOND

2007

CONTENTS

This Book Is Dedicated To Those Who Find Themselves Within Its Pages And To Others Who By Reading My Stories Are Reminded Of Their Own.

WHAT IS YOUR NAME?

My father and I were sitting in the stingy shade of a mesquite tree under a blazing hot July sun in the late 1930s. We were on the banks of the Nolan River in North Central Texas. The Nolan River was named for Phillip Nolan. Nolan was famous for being a Texas patriot who had helped set the stage for Texas' independence from Mexico, but other legends claim he was merely a horse thief killed by Spanish soldiers.

We weren't giving Nolan much thought on that hot afternoon. We had more important matters on our minds. We were sitting by our pickup truck, slapping the pesky flies, waiting to ford his river. The spring rains had washed out the bridge and fording the river in a pickup was a tedious chore. It required the driver to maneuver the truck carefully through the narrowest but shallowest point of the river. The trick was to drive slowly enough so that water didn't splash into the engine's carburetor or distributor since that would cause the motor to die, but fast enough to keep from being swept along sideways by the river's current.

We were sitting by our truck waiting for another to come across the river before taking a turn on the narrow path. When the approaching driver had completed the fording he parked nearby to let the water drain off and to let his racing heart slow down before continuing down the road. He medicated his nerves with a sip of whiskey from a half pint he produced from the back pocket of his overalls.

We fell into an easy conversation with him until I asked, "What is your name?" And then, our easy banter came to an immediate halt. It was as if I had cursed his mother or committed some other mortal sin. "Well," he said, while he paused to wipe his sweaty face with a red bandana, "They call me Red." Of course! His name should have been obvious to me from his red hair and his flushed face. The red bandana was an extra clue. I could have guessed it on a multiple-choice quiz.

Once the man continued on his way and we successfully forded Nolan's river my father explained that rural Texas etiquette did not allow the question, "What is your name?" Instead it was appropriate to ask, "What do they call you?" or, "What do you like to be called?" I later learned that this custom evolved in the area because so many of the early Texas settlers were running from their past and their names. Some of them had come to escape from lawsuits, murders, robberies, or other crimes. Eventually these cases were closed and stamped with the notation: "G. T. T.," meaning "Gone To Texas."

Growing up in Texas I learned almost nothing of my family's name or history. My paternal grandparents had died a few years before I was born and the only thing I knew was that my grandfather had come to Texas from Tennessee. Twenty years later when I was living in Virginia I was struck by the cultural differences. Ancestral worship was a proud way of life in Virginia. It was commonly asked, "Who was your grandfather?" and people there often took pride in their answers to that question.

While in graduate school I found the name of Charles Coffin in a history book. He had come to Tennessee from Massachusetts to teach school and had later become President of a college that eventually became the University of Tennessee. His picture is in the dome of the state Capitol in Nashville.

That bit of information led me to abandon my Texas' cultural prohibition about digging for ancestral roots and I began to look into my family's history. With the help of some work done earlier by a couple of cousins, I traced the Coffin name back through ten generations to when they had arrived in America in 1642. I visited the gravesites of early American Coffins and printed my research in a small book, *Ten Generations of American Coffins,* to share with other family members.

In that project I was able to gather information about names, dates of birth and deaths, children, places of residence, and other facts about the family. But I was missing any sense of what these ancestors were thinking, feeling, and experiencing during those times. I did find a copy of my great, great, great grandfather's diary in The University of Tennessee's Library. Set in the early 18th century, he dutifully recorded the daily weather, which horse he was riding, how many pupils were in his class, along with other details that were probably important to him at the time. But those particulars left me with little sense of what he or others in his time were thinking or feeling about anything.

This introduction is an apology for what follows. My life is certainly not one that warrants the writing of an autobiography. However, I do want to share some stories and memories that are important to me and have helped shape my life. Much of it is happy and some of it may be sad.

Other parts may be boring, but then some of my life has been boring. There are some facts and dates that make up a clothesline on which to hang stories about myself and my friends. Clotheslines aren't common today. Everyone used to have one. They were wires or ropes strung between poles in the backyard. Before the days of indoor dryers people hung their wet laundry to dry outside on these clotheslines. The lines were a laundry necessity but a curse for kids playing Kick the Can or Capture the Flag. Running through the yard at top speed into a neck-high, tight, wire clothesline is a sensation not quickly forgotten. Knowing well both the pleasures and the pains of clotheslines, I want to hang my stories out to dry on my own clothesline.

I woke up this morning wondering how to start this book of stories. I have been struggling with beginning it for some time and today I asked God for some guidance. I wasn't expecting a direct answer. People who talk about hearing God speak to them make me nervous. Those people seem to always hear good news for themselves and bad news for anyone who doubts their experience.

So when I say I talked with God I mean that each morning I spend some time thinking about being in God's presence. This morning during that time I thought about my story-writing problems. I imagined that God's response was something like, "You have been asking me for several days about how I can help you with your writing project. I thought that today we might consider how you can help me instead." Then God started the usual monologue about helping the homeless, the poor, the refugees and the sick. I confess God seems awfully partial to those folks. God concluded by saying, "Just go write your stories."

"I do have a couple of other questions," I added quickly. "Is it all right for me to change some of the names of folks in the stories to protect the guilty? And I notice that when I tell stories, I sometimes exaggerate a bit. Is that okay?"

The Divine response as I understood it was sometime like, "I don't know if it is okay or not but my son Jesus like most story tellers did tend to overstate a bit. Do you remember His talking about a man having not just a speck but a log in his eye? Imagine! A log in your eye? And he talked about faith moving mountains. I guess that story telling and hyperbole tend to go together. Just go write your stories." I wanted to ask more about how to arrange the material but it just didn't seem appropriate to keep God tied up any longer.

So with very little heavenly guidance and a little divine prodding I sat down to work on an outline for my stories. Since it seemed like a fair thing to do I changed the names of most of my living friends in these stories to protect them from embarrassment and me from possible lawsuits.

BIG I AND ME

I grew up in the small town of Itasca in North Central Texas. The town had been established in 1880 as the Kansas-Missouri-Texas Railroad built a line from Ft. Worth to Houston. The company marked off plats along the railroad line for future towns. Legend has it that a railroad mapmaker from Minnesota was working in the Texas heat on a July afternoon laying out the map with the names of towns to be placed about every ten miles along the railroad line. As he dreamed that hot afternoon of being in cool Lake Itasca at the headwaters of the Mississippi River in Northern Minnesota, he could not resist giving the name Itasca to this place on the map.

My grandfather and his two brothers came to Texas from Tennessee and were among the early settlers of Itasca. The town later grew into a farming community of about 1,200 people. Most residents made their living raising cotton and cattle. Some may have thought the town was somewhat backward but in some important ways it was ahead of the times. In 1929 when Wall Street crashed, Itasca was ahead of the curve. Several years before 1929 the price of cotton in Itasca had fallen below the cost of production and the cattle market had bottomed out. The depression had come to our town a few years before the famous stock market crash. It later struck me as ironic that on the outskirts of this depressed community was a large semicircular billboard proclaiming: "ITASCA—The BIG Little Town. Prosper with us."

Itasca: The Big Little Town

There was not much prospering in Itasca in 1929, the year of my birth. I spent my growing up years in Itasca so it was "Big I and Me" until I left for college. One of the stores on the two-block Main Street of our downtown had a sign on the front that read:

J. A. DAVIS AND SONS GROCERY
ESTABLISHED 1919

I may not have the date exactly right but because of that sign I grew up believing that 1919 must have been the beginning of the world. The most prominent building in our town was the cream colored two-story bank building with a red tile roof where my father worked. The building also housed a beauty shop and the barber shop. The bank was located at the intersection of the four blocks that comprised our downtown.

There was a stop sign at that corner where the traffic on the highway from Fort Worth to Waco had to stop before turning west for a block to cross the Missouri-Kansas-Texas Railroad. The highway continued with a turn to the south past the Westside Garage and the cemetery on the way to our county seat of Hillsboro. The town of Itasca, my family, church, school and friends gave me the framework and lens through which I would always view the world. "Big I" left its mark on me in many ways.

Itasca's philosopher was Six Ace. He was the one person your parents, your Sunday school teacher and your scout master told you to avoid. He worked at Pos Hodge's Barber Shop sweeping the floor and doing odd jobs for others including our family. It was rumored he was also a bootlegger meeting the needs of our dry North Texas town. His short-cropped hair was almost white and the crinkles and deep lines in his dark mahogany face made it clear that he had been around for a long time. He either mumbled a lot or was constantly humming to himself. It was hard to tell which. He was always quick with a smile for anyone but we were warned to stay away from him because he was a known gambler.

In our community the evils of gambling were nearly important enough to comprise an eleventh Commandment. We weren't sure about the meaning or significance of the Commandments about bearing false witness and coveting but we clearly understood the evil of gambling. If you gambled with Six Ace he would end up with your money.

He was an all-purpose gambler. He would just as easily take a bet on a World Series game as on the Friday night high school football game. He was equally enthusiastic about placing a bet on the domino game going on in the unofficial men's activity center, the back of the barbershop. Six Ace was even glad to make a wager on which of two flies crawling across the plate glass window in the front of the barber shop would fly away first or at what time the next freight train would come down the track on the west side of our town. He gave credit for his ability to win all these random wagers to Divine guidance. "God talks and Six Ace listens," he would say, as he collected his winnings.

This embodiment of good and evil in the genial old man made him an irresistible attraction to teenage boys. He would tell us stories about the men and women in our town that we could not have heard anywhere else. He may not have been able to repeat all Ten Commandments but he knew adultery, greed and lying when he saw them. Without Six Ace we would not have known about the soap operas occurring in our own town. When we asked our parents about some of these events we began to wonder if the injunctions to stay away from Six Ace were based on their fear of his gambling habits or their fear that he would tell us too much about their lives. He was such a good storyteller and philosopher that despite all the advice we received to the contrary we just couldn't stay away from him. He often told us, "There's just three things that make up life: religion, sex, and money." That seemed like a reasonable framework for life in our town.

Six Ace, a.k.a. Tom, and Me

My introduction to religion came before I was old enough to protect myself. My parents had me baptized as an infant in the Presbyterian Church in Itasca. When I was young I noticed that the Christian cross on the communion table at the front of our church had the letters IHS in the center. I now know that those are the Greek letters for the name of Jesus but at the time I assumed the letters, IHS, stood for "Itasca High School." Later when I saw those same letters in churches in other towns I was pleased but a bit surprised to find that others thought that much of our local high school.

When my Sunday school teacher, Miss Minnie, told me that God was everywhere, all knowing and all-powerful, it wasn't difficult for me to believe. I knew and was known by almost everyone in our little town. When my friend Alex took a package of cigarettes from the shelf of his daddy's drug store and we tried them out behind our chicken house our neighbor saw us and telephoned my mother. Fifteen minutes later when I went in the house to complain of food poisoning, my mother already knew the truth.

One afternoon when the little girl next door and I were about five years old, we were playing doctor in the back of our garage when her older brother saw us. He told his daddy who talked to my daddy who did more than talk to me. By sundown that evening I had lost all interest in the medical profession. If my parents always knew everything I did, it was not difficult for me to believe in a God who was omnipresent. That belief has brought equal parts of comfort and shame to me through the years.

Our religious schedule was rigorous. Sundays included Sunday school, morning worship, youth meetings and evening worship. Tuesday was children's choir practice, and Wednesday evening was our Prayer Meeting. We also had to find time during the week to memorize scripture passages and catechism answers.

My mother sang in the choir on Sunday mornings so I sat next to my father in church. He smelled of Mennen's aftershave and Lucky Strike cigarettes. I grew up believing that God smelled like cigarettes and shaving lotion. Across the wall at the front of our sanctuary was a long row of organ pipes. Each Sunday I would try to count those pipes. It was a difficult task because the pipes tended to run together during the counting process. It helped me count if I held a finger out in front of my eyes and moved it across the row to keep my place. However, while it might have been appropriate in a Pentecostal church to hold a hand out at arm's length with a finger pointed upward, it was not acceptable in our Presbyterian church. When I tried it my mother's disapproving face in the choir would come into view. I was never able to get an accurate count of those pipes.

I wanted to be a deacon. Their responsibilities in our church were to seat the visitors even though we never had any visitors and to take up the collection just before the sermon. That meant that the deacons could stand outside in front of the church and smoke until almost eleven thirty. It seemed like an ideal assignment.

When I was old enough to be released from sitting with my parents I sat with the other young people in a side section of the church. A small Cumberland Church had merged with ours and their small building had been moved to become an addition to the side of our sanctuary. It was an architectural disaster but it was the perfect place for young people to sit because they were out of their parents' sight. That section had a collection of hymnbooks and Bibles with home made puzzles. The first page of the hymnbook would have a note saying, "Turn to page 67." Page 67 would have a note leading to another page and so on until many pages later you would reach the secret message: "Jim likes Louise" or other important news. An X-rated Bible puzzle would lead from one Old Testament passage to another following the risqué stories of Lot and his daughters, David and Bathsheba and other similar sexual passages.

It was difficult for me as a Presbyterian young person to be a part of a religious minority. The Southern Baptists dominated our part of the world. Their huge Southwestern Theological School was just forty-five miles to the north in Ft. Worth and their signature Baylor College was forty-five miles to the south in Waco. We lived directly in the bull's eye between those epicenters of Baptist influence. The Southern Baptists clearly set the religious standards for that part of the country. The embarrassing part for the Presbyterian minority was highlighted by one simple fact. We did not hold revivals. Revivals were an important part of the social fabric of the community and for a church not to hold these events was almost unpatriotic.

We kept asking our parents or the preacher, "Now tell us again why we Presbyterians don't have revivals?" They would give us another mini course in theology entitled The Sovereignty of God and explain again that Presbyterians believe that the important action in the salvation process is God's action in Christ—God's grace. I can still hear the Presbyterian preacher saying, "God chooses us. We do not choose God." While others might emphasize the human response such as accepting the invitation from the evangelist to come down front at the end of a revival service, Presbyterians continue to focus on the Divine action rather than on the human response. That is why our Presbyterian Church does not hold revivals we were told.

That lecture would hold us until the Baptists had their

late summer revival. The event would be scheduled for a week of evenings in late August before school began, when the crops had been laid by and the oppressive heat had exhausted everyone's spirits. This was before the days of air conditioning, so the Baptists put benches out in the side yard of the church hoping to catch a little evening breeze. Lights would be strung up around the area and those would attract flying insects from all over the county. A song leader from Waco and an evangelist from Ft. Worth would also be brought in for the week.

The revival was a great social occasion for most of the community. However the man who ran the shoe repair shop did not enjoy it. His was the only Jewish family in town and during revival week all of the Baptists would stop by to try to convince Mr. Sam to convert. He was not led to make this change and that was probably a good thing. He may have been the last person in town not identified as a Christian and if he had converted, there might not been a need for any further revivals.

I was at one of the revivals the night the evangelist declared that he believed that Presbyterians also needed to be saved. At first it felt to me like a put down but then it took a good turn. There was a young woman in our high school that I had long admired but who would never give me a second glance. She was a Baptist and after hearing the evangelist's declaration about Presbyterians she became very interested in my soul. With my interest in her body we formed a short-lived body/soul relationship. The courtship did not go very far because my roots in the Presbyterian tradition would not let me turn my soul over to the Baptists and my fear of her father limited how much of her body could be explored. I may have lost a girlfriend at the end but it helped me develop an abiding faith in a God who loved and cared for me and all people whether or not we had come down the church aisle at a revival.

I now realize that my worst Sunday school teacher may have been my best. The high school boys' class of five or six met in a small windowless room each Sunday morning. Our teacher, Mr. Hooks, would open the drawer of the little table in the room and pull out the quarterly magazine that contained the lesson. We would pass the magazine around with each of us reading one paragraph until we came to end. He would then put the periodical back in the drawer to wait for the next Sunday. After that we would have a serious conversation about our real religion—football.

Mr. Hooks developed a successful motivational program around our interest in sports. He challenged us to read four chapters in the Bible each day and on Sunday we would have to report that we had completed our daily readings. It was not the kind of thing you wanted to lie about, no matter how tempted you were. If at the end of the year you had completed the four chapters a day you would have read the entire Bible. The prize for us may not have been increased Biblical literacy. The real reward for those who had successfully completed the challenge was that Mr. Hooks would take us to the Cotton Bowl football game in Dallas on New Year's Day. Taking that trip was like taking a trip to the Super Bowl today. There was intense competition and to get those readings in each day required a lot of hard work.

So my Sunday school teacher who never prepared for a lesson lured me into the habit of reading through the Bible each year. I know that reading through the Bible sixty times will not provide me with a pass to heaven. But that practice each morning has left a mark on me. While I have certainly engaged in arguments with God and expressed disapproval of some of God's activities, there has never been a day as far back as my memories will go when I doubted that there is a God who cares about me and this world. That relationship is a part of the fiber of my being.

When Six Ace listed sex as one of the foundations of life I did not realize how profoundly true that was. Sex was not just a physical act. A person's sex or gender also determined the person's status.

I was in college when it occurred to me for the first time that not everyone in the world wanted to be a white male preferably from Texas. In Big I being white meant that you didn't have to live in Freetown, the slum area of dilapidated shacks. Even as a young boy I understood that white males were on the top end of the social scale and that in general, men ruled the world. They ran the businesses, the farms, the families and the churches. There were a few women in our town who held clerical jobs or who worked as school teachers, but ultimately, the men were in charge. I could see that the men were not necessarily better or more capable. It was just the way it had always been. It was just the tradition. A person's gender determined his or her lot in life.

Women certainly had their important roles in the family, in society, in religious life and sometimes in the community's business life. My mother was a good example. She provided us with a wonderful home. She was very active in the life of the church and in other social activities, but because she was a woman, she did not belong to the Chamber of Commerce or

Rotary Club, and she did not serve as a member of the School Board. Six Ace was right. Sex was significant.

To be fair I know Six Ace was referring to more than the gender roles of those times. He also knew about the powerful influence physical and romantic sex exerted over the lives of men and women and boys and girls in our town. While most adults in our town told us that they didn't know why a popular bachelor left town in a big hurry Six Ace explained to us that the bachelor had been 'seeing' the wife of a neighbor. The look in Six Ace's eyes when he told us this juicy piece of gossip let us know that the bachelor had been doing a bit more than seeing the neighbor's wife from across the driveway.

Our schools did not offer any sex education classes but at least we Presbyterians had an advantage over the Baptist teenagers who were encouraged to believe that sex did not exist. Each year our Presbyterian youth group was taught a program on boy-girl relationships. I do not remember the title of the program but the lesson attempted to describe how far it was appropriate to go in "petting." The point was generally, "no touching" below the face. It was a pretty exotic experience for a small town boy. Even without Six Ace's sage advice on the topic I would have guessed that sex was going to be a powerful influence in life.

Six Ace's third category of importance was money. There were a few families in our town that had money. They might not have been considered wealthy outside of our small community, but since everything is relative, they were rich in Big I. My father told me about a local cotton farmer who owned 365 shares of AT&T stock. At the time that stock was paying an annual dividend of a dollar a share. That meant he earned a dollar a day without having to do anything. I could not imagine such luxury.

The merchants and farmers of our town were likely our middle class folks and our family was in that group. But the majority of our town was poor. The poor in our town lived in inadequate housing and did not eat well. The African Americans, about one third of our town's population, fell into that category.

The house where I grew up was built in 1926 just two years after my mother and father were married. The first year they were married they lived with my father's sister, her husband, and their six young children. The second year they lived with my father's Aunt Sallie. She had a reputation for being nosey and ill tempered. What a way to start a marriage. I remember my father saying that the house cost $2,200 to build. It was a fairly small wooden structure and I know that my mother was glad to move into her own home.

A couple of years ago I went by to see the house. It seemed very small by today's standards but it was a comfortable house for the times. The house was heated by natural gas in those days before thermostats and pilot lights. Lighting the stove meant turning on the gas then striking a match and holding it just above the open gas jet. There would be a muffled— POOF—from the small explosion around the hand holding the match as the space heater came to life. You could always tell which member of our family lighted the stove in the winter because that person had no hair on the back of one hand.

We had a comfortable lifestyle but it was not extravagant. We certainly had enough food and clothing but we only went on one family vacation. My father put in long hours as cashier and later as president of the bank, and most days he went to the ranch before the bank opened and after it closed. By the time I started to school I was responsible for feeding the chickens in our backyard and for bringing in the eggs.

When I began high school my father decided that I needed

some added responsibilities, so he set me up in the dairy business. He fenced in a couple of acres across the street from our house, built a small barn, and purchased three milk cows. Before school every morning and every day after school I milked the cows and bottled the milk. My mother and sister occasionally helped me by cleaning the bottles and straining the milk, but milking the cows and bottling the milk took me almost two hours every morning and every afternoon. I also delivered the milk to some residential customers and to the grocery store. The worst part of the dairy business is that there are no holidays or weekends off. I tried to teach my sister to milk and thought that she was a bit retarded when she couldn't learn. Looking back I realize just how smart she was about that.

I also occasionally substituted as a school bus driver. This with the dairy business did provide me with a modest bank account. However I had little use for money. In those days a date on Friday night was not an expensive venture. Two tickets to the movie at nine cents each, popcorn at a nickel a bag, and drinks at the drug store after the movie still left change from a dollar bill. There was nowhere else in our town in the evening to spend money.

If my father thought that the dairy business would make me an ambitious, happy capitalist or lead me to develop an appreciation for farm animals, it did not work. One of the happiest parts of my life was leaving the dairy business when I graduated from high school. Six Ace was correct. Money was definitely important but that dairy business and bus driving taught me that having money and earning money in particular, was not necessarily a satisfying venture. I was grateful to learn that money was only one of Six Ace's three most important things in life.

FAMILY

My mother was born in Pecos, Texas while Judge Roy Bean, the Hanging Judge, was still alive. Her mother died while she was young and her father recognizing that West Texas was not a hospitable place for a child without a mother sent her to Central Texas to be raised by her aunts. She graduated in 1919 from college at Texas Christian University where she was a cheerleader. The College annual for that year has a picture of her as a beautiful, black-haired young woman with a winning smile in her old-fashioned cheerleader's uniform. After college graduation she came to Itasca to be a schoolteacher since teaching was one of the few professions open to women. She met and married my father. A year and a half later, my sister Jane was born.

Jane and I lived in the same house, but we lived in different worlds. She learned to cook and sew, to put on makeup and fix her hair, to read books, and to take school seriously. I learned to ride horses, milk cows, fight, look at girls, and do as little schoolwork as possible. After we became adults Jane and I became very good friends but the culture of our earlier times had us living in separate worlds.

My mother cared for me with great attention and affection. However, I have joked that she also taught me to lie. As a young boy I was nearsighted. Before my mother realized it she would often point out an object and ask if I saw it. She'd say, "Look at that bird in the tree." I would ask, "Where?" She'd point up into the tree and say, "Right there on the branch." After trying to see that bird several times and still just seeing a blurry sky I'd tell her, "Oh, now I see it." I just wanted to make her happy. By lying to please my mother I learned that not telling the truth was all right if it made someone else happy. It wasn't long until I began to believe that lying might be all right if it made me happy.

My mother, "Margie," was well known in our town. She was not flamboyant or showy but she had a lot of different interests. Mother was very involved in the life of our church. She taught a women's Sunday school class for many years and after her death the class was taught by an aunt. Now almost fifty years later the class is still known as the Coffin Bible Class. She sang in the choir and for a period of time when our church didn't have a choir director she took over that task.

Margie was interested in the community. She had been a teacher and understood that hungry children do not learn well. When she found that many of the children from poor families had little to eat for breakfast and did not bring a lunch to school with them, she began to talk about starting a school lunch program. Mother finally went to the School Board to make the proposal. The men rejected her idea. She wasn't bitter about their rejection, but in the following weeks she found an occasion to talk about this need individually with their wives. It wasn't long before the School Board implemented a school lunch program.

In those days, the school for black children was separate and certainly not equal. Mother became concerned about this and began to have conversations with others about the deplorable conditions of the Black School. The school board began to hear complaints and questions. As a result, the board implemented improvements including a lunch program. I think the men on the board moved more quickly this time because they did not want my mother talking to their wives.

Mother was interested in all of life. She was an avid reader and was probably the only person in town who subscribed to a liberal religious journal. I have wondered if she also looked through catalogues because some of the clothes she dressed me in were certainly not available locally.

She loved music as well. She had learned to play the piano as a child while living with her aunt and uncle. They had a wonderful foot-operated player piano. Perforated rolls of paper were put into holders on the face of the piano, and when the pedals were pumped, the rolls of paper turned and the piano played beautiful music. By watching the keys depress and holding her fingers on them my mother leaned to play the piano.

She played ragtime music very well which wasn't a surprise since most of the music rolls in her Aunt's house came from that era. She also played hymns with great feeling. Some evenings she would sit at the piano in our house and play ragtime or other popular music and then move on to hymns. There were moments when she seemed to be in another world. She was a deeply religious person and at times her music seemed part of a mystic experience. We did not try to talk to her during those periods of obvious reverence.

I learned a lot about God's love from Mother as I saw her love for Him. I knew that she loved God with her heart by watching her in those mystical moments with her music. She also loved God with her mind. After she died we found hundreds of pages of material that she had prepared through the years of her Bible studies. She loved God with her strength as well and demonstrated that love as she reached out to the needs of children and others in our community.

My father was born in Itasca five years before the end of the nineteenth century. His father and grandfather had both been named John McKinney Coffin and that name continued for five generations through my name and my son's name. The home my father built for his wife was on a lot across the street from the house where he was born. He lived and died on the same street. Itasca was truly his home.

He had been to other parts of the world. Joining the Marine Corps at the beginning of World War I, he saw action in France and Germany. The mustard gas used by the Germans caused him respiratory problems the rest of his life. After coming home from the war, he returned to Texas and for a brief time worked in the notoriously rough and dangerous oil fields of East Texas. Returning to Itasca he spent as few nights as possible away from his hometown.

As a cashier and then as the bank president my father provided our family with financial security but banking was not his first choice for a career. His true loves were farming and ranching. He owned a ranch twenty miles or so west of Itasca and a smaller farm east of our town. A visit to the ranch or farm was routine for him before banking hours in the morning or in the afternoon after the bank closed. Because of his dedication to those farms fifteen-hour days were not unusual for him.

Church and civic affairs were also important to him. Along with the banking and ranching business he was an avid trader. He enjoyed buying, selling, and trading land, produce, livestock, machinery and almost anything else.

I remember going with him one Saturday morning to meet a couple of buyers from Ft. Worth who were interested in purchasing some sheep. It was a hot morning and we had neglected to bring along our canteen of water, a rule we seldom broke. While waiting for the men we were chewing mesquite leaves. There was a theory that this would quench your thirst but I believe that the bitter taste of the leaves only changed the subject.

The sheep waiting to be shown to the buyers were in a wooden board pen near the barn. After the men from Ft. Worth arrived we stood with each of us having a foot resting on one of the planks in the customary stance, a toe of the boot sticking through the fence. The usual trading conversational foreplay began to take place.

"What do you want for the sheep?" one of the traders asked.

My father volleyed back with the question, "What will you give me?"

The trader then offered a price. I do not remember the offer he made but after it was spoken my father did not immediately reply. After a pause, in an excited voice he cried out, "Jump back! Quick!" We assumed that he was warning us of a rattlesnake about to strike since they were common in that area. We rapidly jumped away from the pen and looked around. After seeing no danger we all looked at my father wondering what the emergency was. Turning to the buyers he said, "I don't want you fellers even looking at those sheep. Might hurt their feelings with that low an offer." It was just one of his trader's ploys. They finally settled on an agreeable price.

One time he bought, sight unseen, a railroad car of wild horses from Arizona. I do not remember exactly how many horses were in that car but there must have been sixty or seventy. Some of them went straight to the glue factory. Others he sold to folks locally. We kept a dozen or so and spent weeks breaking the best ones for riding. In fact one broke me. After being thrown from one of the wild horses I was hospitalized.

Once I was discharged I spent several weeks on my back in bed unable to turn because of the injuries. This was before the days of air conditioning and the summer heat assured that I was miserable. When I finally left that bed I was convinced that I was not destined to be a roughneck cowboy. I did learn to play the harmonica during that time of confinement and it was clear to me also that I was not going to be a great musician.

My father was not a very sentimental person and I seldom felt comfortable using "Daddy" or other more informal titles for him. In my early years, we both disappointed each other. He must have wanted me to be a big strong boy who loved ranching and the land. I felt inadequate in the face of those expectations and spent a lot of time daydreaming about another life. We did not have a close warm relationship but there was no hostility or antagonism between us. We were just interested in different worlds.

As the husband and breadwinner, my father worked hard to provide financial security for his family and he succeeded during some difficult times. I learned a lot of things from him about hard work, honesty, and integrity. He was well respected and an active part of our community. Let me share a story to give you a feel for his character.

While money may have been important to my father he did have some higher values. He loved the ranch he owned along the Nolan River, a tributary of the Brazos River. The Army Corp of Engineers made plans to build a dam on the Brazos River that would create a large lake. Part of my father's ranch would be flooded and additional acreage would be in the flood plain. Obviously my father was not happy about the plan. He received a letter informing him of the dam to create Lake Whitney and offering money to compensate for the loss of his land. He threw the letter away without responding. He repeated this pattern with several pieces of mail that came during the next few months. He refused to sign for registered letters or make any official response. He ignored the fact that the land was being condemned under the rights of eminent domain.

One afternoon I was sitting with my father in his bedroom where his various health problems guaranteed that he spend a good part of his time. Out the window we saw a black sedan stop in front of the house. Three men in suits and ties got out of the car. Slowly they walked to the front door. "It's the Government," he said. No one in our town drove a big black sedan or went visiting wearing suits and ties on weekdays in the summer. No one came to the front door. Ever! Not even the preacher.

I went out to meet them and ignoring all our traditional rites of courtesy did not invite them into the house. The leader of the group stepped forward and told me that he had come from the office in St. Louis to have John Coffin sign some papers. He did not introduce himself or offer to shake hands. Since I had not invited them into the house, we were even with each other in ignoring the rites of common courtesy. He explained that he could not believe my father's arrogance in not responding to several letters and that he had made the long trip to settle the matter.

To play for a little time I introduced myself and shook hands with the other two men. One of them was a lawyer from Ft. Worth and the second one was some kind of a security or law enforcement officer. I then announced that my father was not well and would not be coming to the door. With that news, the head honcho announced that they would just go inside to see my father. I asked them to wait on the porch while I went in to check on that plan. I was not surprised when my father told me in rather colorful language that he was not interested in seeing the visitors.

When I returned to the front porch with this news the leader's face flushed and he announced, "Well, we will just go in and speak to him anyway, because he is going to sign these papers now." He started to push me aside and gain entrance to the door when the lawyer caught his arm to stop him. I could not hear what the lawyer said, but it obviously had something to do with entering a house without permission.

The leader then turned to me and held out a sheaf of papers and said, "I am delivering these papers to you and they are to be signed and sent back to us by return mail." I kept my arms at my side. In frustration the man dropped the papers to the floor of the porch and marched back toward the car. On many occasions I have cursed the persistent south wind in the summer and north wind in the winter that blew incessantly across the plains of North Central Texas. I was so proud of the wind that afternoon. It picked up the pile of papers that Mr. Big Shot had dropped at my feet and scattered those documents into our front yard. It then floated them across the street and laid them to rest in front of the visitors' car as it left.

A few years later my father died. In his will he had named Jane and me as the executors and sole beneficiaries of his estate. When we opened his safe deposit box at the bank we found a check from the U.S. Government for several thousand dollars for the land lost to the ranch by the floodwaters of Lake Whitney. Obviously the government had finally used the powers of eminent domain to acquire the property and paid my father what it had determined as the fair market value for the land. Daddy's last act of defiance was to not cash the check.

Jane and I debated what we should do. Should we uphold his rebellion and destroy the check or should we cash it? We decided that he must not have thought that it was necessary for us to uphold his principle or he would have destroyed the check. Instead he left it for us assuming that one generation of rebellion was enough. At least that was the rationale we used for taking the money. While my father appreciated the value of money he knew that some things were even more important, such as his love for his ranch.

Daddy's love of the land and hard work to provide for his family, his demanding honesty for himself and others, and his unwavering loyalty to his values even when he was weak and sick were remarkable traits. Those characteristics help me appreciate the Christian God I worship and adore, who tirelessly works for justice, who exhibits loyalty and truth, and whose love never gives up on us.

My mother's deep love and high spirits were a good balance for my father's rough style and self-assurance. I was fortunate to receive from my parents that nice combination of tough, no-nonsense security and warm, high-spirited love.

Daddy, Mom, and Me, in funky pajamas

My sister Jane was just two years older than I was but we
lived in two very different worlds. My world was one of horses,

cows, sports, work, play, and the outside world. Jane learned to cook and sew, play the piano, read books, and listen to good music. She was a serious student and pushed herself to earn the best grades. Being proper, doing things right, and striving to be the best were important goals for her. How a brother and sister living in the same house growing up only two years apart in age could have had so little in common is amazing to me. I had to work to try to bring some chaos and fun into her organized world.

There was one incident about which I still feel some guilt and shame. Jane had graduated from Texas Christian University in Ft. Worth and The Presbyterian School of Christian Education in Richmond, Virginia. She was teaching school in Stanton, Virginia when she became engaged to Bill, who was studying for the ministry. They were to be married in Itasca that summer. It was early June and I was out of school and at home for a few days for the wedding.

Two days before the event we were waiting for the arrival of Bill, his parents, and a sister who were riding the train to Texas from North Carolina. That afternoon a friend and I were looking for something to do when one of us came up with a funny plan. We went to the railroad depot and had our friend who worked there make up a fake telegram. It said:

"Dear Jane, I have had a change of heart and will
not be coming for the wedding. Letter follows. Bill"

We took the telegram to my house, slipped it under the front door, rang the doorbell, and sped away before we were seen. We then became interested in something else and forgot about our prank.

When I walked into the house for supper that night I

could feel a heavy pall in the air. Jane was in tears and mother was trying to console her. At that moment I remembered the fake telegram. In the face of the disastrous results of my prank my first temptation was to run away from home and join the merchant marines. I quickly confessed and hoped to see Jane's sadness turn to relief and joy. Instead, it turned into anger and disbelief that I would have created such a hoax. I finally received her undeserved forgiveness and see it now as proof of how much she loved her foolish younger brother.

She had plenty of occasions to show her acceptance and love for me in the future. For a number of years my family lived in Nashville, Tennessee, and at least twice a year we made the trip to Texas to visit our parents. This was before the days of interstate highways and the trip was a long adventure with our five children. Jane and her husband Bill were thoughtful enough to choose to live in Arkansas. Their house was on our route from Nashville to Dallas. Going to and from Texas we spent nights with them. They were gracious hosts to the two adults and five children who descended on them for room and board year after year. It was a test of true love. We became very close friends.

As a boy one of my responsibilities was to bring in the laundry from the clothesline. A woman I called "Miss Minnie" came to our house every Monday morning to wash our clothes, sheets, and towels. The washhouse was a small shed behind our house that had a wide bench and a few washtubs. There was cold water running to the shed and a large wash kettle outside nearby. A wood fire heated the water in the early years. Later natural gas was piped to it. The laundry was washed in lye soap made with the lard my mother saved from pork cooked for our dinners. Twice a year the lard was melted and lye was added to make soap. The clothes were soaked in the big kettle of hot water with the soap and then were scrubbed on a washboard. After the scrubbing the clothes were rinsed in tubs of clean water and the shirts and pants were dipped in starch water. The laundry was then hung on the clotheslines in the back yard. It was pretty labor-intensive work compared to today's washers and dryers.

It was my job to bring in the clothes on Monday afternoon after they had dried in the Texas sun and wind. One afternoon however, I was playing at a friend's house and forgot my chore. To add to the crime a late afternoon shower had soaked the dried clothes. My punishment was a few swats on my bottom from my father using his razor strop.

Modern inventions changed a lot of things. My father started using the newly created safety razor and the strop was gone. We also acquired a stand-up washing machine with a hand-powered wringer. Miss Minnie and I welcomed modern technology with enthusiasm.

SCHOOL

The building where I went to school from the first through the eleventh grade was about three blocks from our house so I walked home for lunch every day. The noon meal was dinner at our house. It was our big meal of the day but we did not eat it together as a family during the school year. I came home from school for lunch at 11:30, Jane at noon, and my father from the bank at 12:30. Since each of us had thirty minutes for lunch we seldom were at the table at the same time. Why did my mother put up with that?

I didn't hate school, but I didn't love it either. The academic work was not too difficult for me, but I did have some problems in the first grade before teachers and my parents recognized that I was nearsighted and couldn't see the letters on the blackboard. In our town the jewelry store had an eye chart, and the owner knew how to order glasses. So we ordered a pair from him for me.

I hated wearing the glasses. No one else in our class wore glasses and of course I was called "Four Eyes." I also stood out in the class because during the winter months I wore corduroy knickers and lace up boots. I had respiratory problems during cold weather and the doctor told my mother to dress me warmly. Not only did I look strange but the swishing sound my corduroys made when I walked ensured that I sounded funny too. I knew that my mother loved me but it was difficult to believe when she put me in that awkward situation.

In the seventh grade I had my first real love affair. It began on the first day of school when our new teacher walked into the room and introduced herself as Miss Trimble. She had just graduated from college and had come to our small town from the city. She was beautiful and my heart began to beat in 6/8 time.

That afternoon after school I knew that I had to express my affection for Miss Trimble with a present. What did a thirteen-year old boy have to give? Since one of my jobs was to care for the chickens in the pen behind our house I did have some young fryers that had hatched out in the early summer. I choose the plumpest one and holding it tightly by the neck, wrung off its head as I had been trained to do. I put it in a paper bag and with pride walked the three blocks to the house where Miss Trimble had a rented room and took her meals.
I was nervous when I knocked on her door and speechless when she opened the door. I proudly held out the paper bag holding the dead chicken. By then the blood had oozed out on the side of the bag. She looked at it with horror. I mumbled, "This is a present for you," and laid it on the floor. My feet led me off of the porch and back home as I was feeling pleasure about my gift. Miss Trimble may have been overwhelmed by it but now I know that it was not with joy. She probably had never seen a fresh, headless chicken.

Her first retaliation for my misunderstood kindness may have been that spring when there was a county meet for all of the schools in the area. In the morning there were athletic contests. I ran for our school in the relay race. We might have won if I had not dropped the baton when it was passed to me on the second lap. The afternoon contests were the debates and speaking events. Miss Trimble had entered me in the declaration section that called for individuals to memorize and recite poems or speeches. She had me recite a poem by Oliver Wendell Holmes that I believe he had written for his 50th Harvard school reunion. Imagining that the old men who were at the reunion were young again the poem began:

"Has ever a man got mixed with the boys?
If he has, throw him out without making a noise.
Hang the almanac cheat, the catalogue spite,
Old time is a liar, we are twenty tonight.
We are twenty! We are twenty! Who says we are more?
He's a tipsy young jackanape, Show him the door.
Grey temples at twenty? Yes, white if we please.
Where snow falls the thickest nothing can freeze."

The poem goes on verse after verse and I recited it without a clue about what any of it meant. What could a young boy who did not yet have a whisker understand about old men wanting to play like they were young again? It was not a surprise that I did not place in the event.

The first place winner was a senior in high school who announced before he began his recitation that at the end of the year he was going into military service. The year was 1942, only a few months after the attack on Pearl Harbor and patriotism was running like a fever across the country. I do not remember what he recited. It may have been the Declaration of Independence or the Gettysburg Address. It would not have mattered if he had told a Mother Goose story. National loyalty would have made him a winner during those patriotic days.

A beautiful and charming fifteen-year-old girl won second place. She recited a semi-religious poem that began with:

"Abou Ben Adam, may his tribe increase,
Awoke one night from a sweet dream of peace.
And saw, within the moonlight of his room,
Making it rich, and like a lily in bloom,
An angel writing in a book of gold."

The poem goes on to talk about the angel speaking to Mr. Ben Adam. Since religion was second only to patriotism in our county the young woman would have won even if she had not had the appearance of an angel standing on that stage. I did not come anywhere near placing in the contest and was embarrassed by the whole event. My suspicion was that Miss Trimble was paying me back for the chicken incident.

There was one other similar event. At the end of the school year when Miss Trimble was returning to the city, never to be seen again in our town, she gave us her new address. Impatiently I waited several days before writing her a letter. I did not want to seem too eager. Finally I wrote to her, and was disappointed not to receive a reply for several weeks. One day a letter from her came in the afternoon mail. It is difficult to believe that in those days the post office delivered mail to our homes twice a day! I opened the letter with great anticipation. What a disappointment! I discovered that the envelope contained only the letter I had written to her. She had carefully marked with a red pencil my grammatical and spelling mistakes as if it had been a homework paper I had turned in at school. My first love affair was over.

One of the things that I did not like about school was that the teachers had total control over the students. The teacher told us when to sit and where to sit, when to stand, to speak or to be quiet. Something about my need for independence made that an almost unacceptable situation for me. During my last three years of high school an opportunity to express my independence developed. The years were 1943-1946 and all of the able-bodied men were away in the military. Itasca had a volunteer fire department so we high school boys were recruited for this task. On top of one of the buildings downtown was a loud siren that served as the fire alarm. Our school was only a few blocks from downtown and the alarm could easily be heard from there. When the alarm sounded during school hours those of us who were volunteer firemen could immediately jump up from our desks without permission. We would race out of the classroom, down the two flights of stairs, and run for the firehouse. It was a liberating experience. We wished for even more fires in our town.

In those days, the State of Texas mandated only eleven years of public school. Three months after my sixteenth birthday my high school graduation day arrived. I do not remember much about the graduation ceremony but I can vividly remember one part of it. A Baptist preacher had been invited to deliver the sermon. As he preached he kept raising the sleeve of his coat and looking toward the cuff of his shirt. I assumed he was looking at his watch and I felt good about it since it seemed to me that most preachers cared very little about the time when they were preaching or they would have stopped much earlier.

The preacher, who was not using a manuscript, finally explained that he had nine points to his sermon. He had written those points on the cuff of his shirt so that he would not forget any. After twenty-five minutes he revealed that he was on his second point. The audience collectively shuddered realizing how much more was to come. I do not recall any of the points today but that shirt cuff made a strong impression. A few days after graduation, I took my Big I education off to college.

EXTENDED FAMILY

My father's older sister, her husband, and their six children lived two blocks from our house. Their house was a second home to me. When I was small anytime Mother was going to be away, I was parked at Aunt Janie's. It was a pretty exciting place to be. The two boys and four girls in her family were all several years older than I was and their home was a flurry of activity.

There was a bowl of orange marmalade that stayed in the middle of their large kitchen table. If no one was looking it was possible to walk by and dip two fingers of delicious, sweet marmalade into your mouth without being caught. No such sweets were available around the clock at our house.

Aunt Janie also had an exciting piece of equipment with a fancy name that I can no longer remember. It was a box-like structure used to look at special photographs through a double set of lenses. The results produced a wonderful three-dimensional effect with fascinating pictures from around the world. It was not television. That was still some decades in the future but it was good entertainment.

These two pleasures could not begin to compare with the thrill of their family's subscription to *National Geographic* magazine.

This allowed a young child to sit in the corner for hours engaged in what appeared to be a study of the geography and cultures of the world. In fact, the fascination was in the pictures of the bare breasted and scantily clad women in Asia and Africa. It may have been the only pornography in our town, and it held me spellbound. I never minded spending afternoons at Aunt Janie's.

When I was a teenager, my cousin Paul, who was my age, moved to Itasca with his family when his father died. It was like having a brother and we were close friends. We fought, played, and worked together.

We had an aunt who had left Texas as a young woman and moved to New York City where she taught piano for all of her adult life. One of the family treasures was that each summer she invited two of her nieces or nephews to come to New York to spend the summer with her. Paul and I were invited one summer in the early 1940s. We were probably twelve years old and I now wonder at our parents' judgment in letting us make that journey. I had been to Ft. Worth, forty-five miles from Itasca, and that was my primary experience with the outside world. This was my first trip on a bus or train.

Paul and I rode the bus to Ft. Worth and caught the train to St. Louis where we changed trains for New York. This was during World War II, and the trains were packed with soldiers. The engines were coal fired and the passenger cars were not air-conditioned. The windows were lowered in the passenger cars and when the train went through tunnels the cars filled with coal smoke.

I had never seen such crowds of people. As we were approaching New York City two days later we were apprehensive about finding our aunt in the crowds of people. The conductor came through the car announcing our approaching arrival by calling out, "New York, New York". We excitedly gathered our suitcases and jumped off of the train as it arrived at the station. We looked around and there was no sign of our aunt.

Just before the train pulled out one of us noticed a sign reading, "Newark". We had gotten off a station too soon because the conductor's strange Yankee accent calling out "Newark" had sounded like "New York" to us. Fortunately we were able to get back on the train just as it was pulling out and we made it to Pennsylvania Station, the next stop, where we did find our aunt. If we had not made it back on the train I guess we would have spent the rest of our lives in New Jersey.

It was a wonderful summer learning to ride the subways and visiting all the sites. I disappointed my aunt by saying that I thought that the Brazos River in Texas was prettier than the Hudson River. She was also chagrined when my homesickness made us return home before the summer was over.

On our way home she went with us on the train as far as Washington, D. C. We spent the day visiting the historical national sites. It was a rainy day and she hired a taxi to drive us around. When we came to the Jefferson Memorial there was a heavy rain shower and we decided not to get out of the cab. With a straight face she told us that the Jefferson Memorial was to honor Jefferson Davis. For years I thought it was so generous of the nation to honor the leader of the Confederacy. My Southwestern history lessons had led me to believe that Jefferson Davis was at least as important as Thomas Jefferson for whom the monument had really been established.

Paul's mother bought a ranch near Itasca and my father tried to give us some experience in the cattle business. We had one adventure that left a strong impression on Paul and me. It was a scorching hot July day when my father sent us to look for some cattle that had managed to break a fence and wander off of our ranch near the little town of Blum, Texas.

Early that morning Paul and I loaded our horses in a

trailer and went to search for the cattle. We drove to an area west of our ranch where the Brazos River made a big bend leaving a large area of several square miles of isolated land. On horseback we followed a trail up into this wilderness and finally came to a shack sitting in an open area surrounded by cedar and mesquite trees. We stopped some distance from the house and called out the customary "Hello to the house" that was used as a long distance doorbell in most rural areas. An old man and a younger man came out to the porch and signaled us to approach. As we rode up to the porch, two women came out of the house with three small children clutching the women's flour sack skirts.

It was obvious from the red eyes of the women and the subdued nature of the men that something was wrong. The old man told us that during the night a baby had died and he asked us if we would dig a grave for the dead child's body. It was not what we had in mind for the day but of course we agreed. We tied our horses in the shade of a tree and went to the back of the house where we were given a pick, a shovel, and a heavy iron bar to break and pry up rocks. They pointed us to a place behind the house past the garden on the side of hill where we were to dig the grave.

For the next hour or so we labored in the hot sun clearing out a hole that we thought would be wide and long enough but certainly would not have met the six feet deep standard. The old man came out to inspect our work and flew into a rage. "Don't you boys know nothing 'bout digging graves?" he bellowed. "Don't you know that graves always face the East?" On reflection I could remember that all of the graves in our family cemetery plot did run east and west. I later learned that it was a Christian custom in those days to bury people facing east towards Jerusalem.

Paul and I spent the next couple of hours filling up the

first grave and digging another one facing the proper direction. After it had passed the old man's inspection the rest of the family came out and stood around the grave. We watched as the dead child's father placed the small body wrapped in an old olive drab blanket into the grave.

The old man signaled for us to stand near the grave. He told Paul to say something. Paul's face turned white and then red. When he finally found his voice he said to the man, "What?" The man sternly answered, "I said you need to say something—like some words at a funeral."

There was a long silence. Paul finally opened his mouth, and these words came out

> "On my honor I will do my best,
> To do my duty to God and my country,
> To obey the Scout Law;
> To help other people at all times;
> To keep myself physically strong,
> Mentally awake, and morally straight."

Why the Boy Scout Oath came to Paul's mind at that moment I do not know. It may sound somewhat religious but it is hardly suitable for a funeral. Paul certainly knew some Scripture such as the words of the Twenty Third Psalm: "The Lord is my shepherd, I shall not want." That would have been much more appropriate. But before I cast any stones let me relate what happened next.

The old man then turned to me and said, "Now you say something". Following Paul's lead the words that poured out of my mouth were:

> "A Scout is trustworthy, loyal, helpful, friendly,
> courteous, kind, obedient, cheerful, thrifty,

brave, clean and reverent."

My reciting the Boy Scout Law was not exactly appropriate in the situation either, but it was what came to mind. The old man's response was, "Well, 'twernt much, but I guess it'll have to do. Now let's fill up the grave."

We did fill the grave, did not find the lost cattle, and went home at the end of the day a lot older than when we had left that morning. Holding funerals will age you in a hurry. We did not talk about it when we returned home but it was a memorable experience for both of us.

Visions of that day returned to my mind in December 1952 when I stood in the Itasca cemetery as Paul's body was lowered into the ground. He had graduated from Texas A & M that spring having been trained to manage the family ranch. At the end of the summer, he was the best man at my wedding and later that fall was sent to Korea where he was killed within a few weeks. My heart was as heavy as the dark winter clouds that hung over the cemetery that cold winter afternoon.

Paul's Mother, Vesta, was a remarkable woman. Earlier she was deeply hurt by the untimely death of her husband. He was a highly successful executive in the petroleum industry in Amarillo. After his death she moved to Itasca where in spite of her sorrow she bravely faced life with vigor. One of my memories of her is from the wedding day of one of her daughters. The wedding was to take place in their home, one of the larger, nicer homes in our town. The day of the wedding the guests had arrived and the house was filled with people. Aunt Vesta had acquired a couple of big field dogs and they had become excited by the wedding crowd. They began to howl loudly outside the door. While it brought some amusement to the crowd it did not provide the proper atmosphere of respect for a wedding.

Aunt Vesta decided to take control of the situation. Coming out of the master bedroom that was doubling that day as the bride's dressing room, she stormed through the living room. Arriving at the front door she pulled up her long, beautiful mother-of-the-bride dress from Neiman Marcus, displaying the cowboy boots she wore underneath. She whistled up the dogs. They jumped in the bed of her pickup, and she drove them five miles out in the country where she made them get out of the truck. After her speedy drive back to town the wedding began. The dogs raced back home, and arrived just in time for their howls to accompany the benediction and become a part of the celebration.

Several years ago my wife Lou Alice and I made a visit to Texas and went to Itasca for a visit. It was a Sunday morning and we went to the Presbyterian church for worship and saw some old friends. After worship we went to my cousin Janie's house for lunch. Along with Janie's husband Ollie, her children and grandchildren, we had a wonderful lunch and begin retelling old stories. One of our favorite stories was about the time Janie's mother, my Aunt Vesta, went to a funeral with Mae Dodson. Mae and her husband Homer ran the Rainbow Café that also served as the Greyhound Bus Station in Itasca. Both Mae and her husband Homer were wonderful advertisements for their café since each of them must have weighed about 300 pounds.

After the funeral Aunt Vesta and Mae went to the cemetery on the edge of town for the burial. As the crowd was gathering it began to rain. Aunt Vesta and Mae decided to edge up to the front of the crowd and find a shelter from the rain under the tent set up for the family near the grave. As they waited for the casket to be brought from the hearse and the burial service to begin, the water from the rain began to run along the ground under the tent.

There are various accounts of exactly what happened next. Was Mae pushed by her friend Vesta? Had she stumbled or had the rain made the ground slick causing her to slip? Whatever the cause Mae fell into the open grave. There were some attempts to pull her up but it was clear that they would pull her arms off before her huge body came up out of the ground. There was some talk about digging a slanting pathway down into the grave so that she could walk out but other burial sites surrounded the open grave so there were obvious problems with that solution.

Then two ingenious young men, Curtis and GC, had a brilliant idea. They drove to the cotton gin a few hundred yards up the highway. In the yard behind the gin were bales of cotton and a tripod of four by fours standing six feet high that would hold scales over a bale of cotton to be weighed. They put the tripod in the back of the pickup and brought it back to the cemetery. Behind the seat of the pickup they had a block and tackle with ropes used to lift heavy objects. They set the tripod up over the open grave, put a thick board on the heavy rope and lowered it into the grave. Mae sat on the board and with the ropes she was hoisted up out of the grave. That image comes to my mind each Easter as we sing the hymn, "Up from the Grave He Arose".

After the story was told that Sunday afternoon, one of Janie's children asked, "Who was the funeral for?" We had to confess that we could not remember but we certainly remembered Mae coming up from the grave. Aunt Vesta did bring color and excitement to our town. My life was surrounded by aunts, uncles, cousins, and others who may not have been related by blood but who were definitely a part of the Itasca Clan.

THE WIDENING CIRCLE

The seven of us were sitting around an old Army blanket on the floor in a large second-floor dormitory room. College was a life-changing event for me. My world was expanding to a circle that included Austin College, a small Presbyterian school in Sherman, Texas, a town just over a hundred miles to the north of Itasca. The year was 1946. Early that morning I had ridden to college with Wayne who had just been discharged from the Army. He was twenty-seven years old and I was seventeen. We rode in the new Ford that he had purchased with his earnings from gambling on the troop ship coming home from Europe.

There were fewer than 100 students enrolled in Austin College that summer so it did not take us long to register. That afternoon we were hanging out in the men's dormitory where we had met a few of the other students, many of whom were army veterans. Wayne suggested a game of poker. I had never played the game. Wayne gave me a crash course in poker playing and told me to sit next to him and to bet only when he mentioned the word "Itasca". We had played just a few hands when a man in a suit with a sour look on his face came in with an authoritative announcement. Gambling was not allowed on this Christian campus and we were all immediately expelled. It flashed through my mind that I had left home that morning and could be back home before dark, completing my college career during the daylight hours of only one summer day.

The man expelling us was the vice president of the college. He reached down, scooped up the money that was on the blanket, and put it in his coat pocket. Wayne slowly stood up to face The Suit. His hands then flashed forward. One of his hands firmly grasped the man's lapel and the other hand grabbed the man's tie pulling their faces six inches apart. With some rather colorful language Wayne explained that being expelled was not a big deal for him. However, he could not remember anyone taking the money from his poker pot and being able to walk away.

The intruder quickly had a change of heart and decided that since we were new and didn't know the rules we would not be expelled. He almost tore the pocket off of his coat retrieving the money and putting it back on the blanket. My college career was saved.

One of my friends from college days talks about what a great place it was because we had the chance to become socialized. I am not sure what he means exactly but I do know the servicemen taught me some things. I learned to smoke and drink beer. I also developed some rather colorful language and a total disregard for rules and customs. The question that was appropriate for any rule, was, "What is the penalty for breaking this rule?" You could only know if it was worth following if you knew the price for breaking it.

After a few weeks at college I had some second thoughts about being there. I think that they call it homesickness. In one of those moments I made my only long distance telephone call home during my college days. When my father answered the telephone I told him that I was not very happy with college life. After a long silence he asked two questions, "Have you paid for your room and board for the summer?" I replied that I had. "Is it paid for anywhere else?" he asked. When I said,

"No," his reply was, "Then I believe you should stay there and get what you paid for".

As I look back I see that I ended up getting more than I paid for. I held several jobs while at college. I was responsible for daily cleaning of the building that housed the administrative offices, the library, and the chapel. I also had the task of nightly turning on the campus floodlights and for turning them off each morning. I guess that electric timers had not yet been invented.

The men's dormitory was heated with radiators connected to an old coal furnace in the basement that had been converted to natural gas. There was no thermostat on the system but there was a pressure gauge next to the boiler. I had the job of lighting the furnace in cold weather and of keeping an eye on the pressure gauge during the day to make certain that the pressure stayed within safe limits. That task required me to check the pressure gauge every hour or so during the cold days and nights and to turn the gas jet up or down to control the pressure and the heat. It was a miracle that the furnace did not blow up and destroy the dormitory. I attended school during two summers and during those summers found work on the crew remodeling the dormitory. I also did some landscaping work. Even with my summertime work schedule life at college seemed easier than my life had been in Itasca.

I desperately wanted to be a chapel counter but never acquired that position. At the time students were required to attend chapel three days a week and each student had an assigned seat. Chapel counters were assigned a section of seats in the chapel to check for any vacancies and to report the names of any students who were not in their assigned seat. Repeated non-attendance could result in expulsion from school. What made the chapel counter's job so attractive was that for a fee a counter might be persuaded to overlook a vacant seat and to not report the absent student. I never secured that lucrative position, so my moral integrity was not tested.

During college days my job and social life were much more important to me than my studies. I was really interested in only a couple of courses. A philosophy course opened a whole new world to me. I had learned in Itasca that there were only two ways to think about things: the right way and the wrong way. My father, the church, and the school all reinforced that idea. To learn that it was possible to see things from different perspectives and that truth was not always one sided was a liberating concept. Even the law could be interpreted in different ways. This newfound flexibility led me to consider going to law school but I never received the application materials I requested and my interest faded before I could order an application again.

I took a class in geology that I found fascinating. It was so interesting that I wanted to take more but the school didn't offer any others. Because of my interest however I was allowed to be the lab assistant the next year and I learned a bit more in that position. If the school had provided additional geology courses I might have become a successful geological engineer growing wealthy in the Texas petroleum business. I might also be in prison for fraud or other felonies.

I spent a lot of my time in college learning to beat the academic system and do well on exams. Rather than simply trying to learn the material I spent a lot of time deciding what questions would be asked on exams. I had also developed the ability to memorize large amounts of material that I could reproduce on an exam. That system earned me top marks in almost all of my courses although it did little to enrich my knowledge of those subjects.

I was very industrious during my college years but on the day before my graduation I learned that the college did not appreciate my industriousness. I was called to the business manager's office. He informed me that they had reviewed my accounts and found that during my college career I had earned more money from the school than I had paid for my tuition, room, and board. He told me that unless I paid the school the difference of $815 I would not be awarded my diploma. I persuaded the dean that I had not been informed of any such rule. The business manager was overruled and I did not have to pay any money to receive my diploma.

While I was certainly happy to earn that diploma it wasn't the best thing I received from college. Early in my freshman year I met a young woman named Lou Alice who captured my heart, mind, and body with the force of a Texas tornado. Until the returning veterans bent the rule it was not appropriate to marry until one had finished school. We waited for five long years but it was clear from the start where our relationship was going.

Lou Alice 1946

College life was an enjoyable and broadening experience for me. I did not have any clear vocational directions but knew that I was not cut out to follow my father in banking and ranching. So what did my future hold?

I have seldom thought of God as being mean spirited but it does seem that the Divine nature has a very playful side. By my last year of school I had decided that I was supposed to become a Presbyterian minister. How amused God must have been to watch someone who had a great distaste for school choose a future that required an additional three years of graduate studies. So after graduation I headed for a theological seminary. I did not hear the loud and clear call from God that some of my friends in the ministry described. It was more of a nudge.

The preachers I had known in my youth were not very attractive types. Small towns did not attract the most popular preachers and many of our ministers were retired or nearing retirement. They just didn't appeal to young people. However one Sunday when I was a very young boy the guest preacher at our church was Dr. Thomas Currie, then the president of Austin Presbyterian Theological Seminary. As I was coming out of church at the end of the service he was standing in the doorway shaking hands with the members of the departing congregation. When I came by he looked me in the eye and putting his hand on my head asked, "Have you ever thought that you might become a minister?" It was such a peculiar and far fetched question that it stuck in my mind. Had he asked me if I had ever considered running away and joining the circus or the French Foreign Legion I would not have been more surprised. I now know that one of the things seminary presidents do is recruit students and Dr. Currie may have been taking that long-range approach with me then. But I confess that it made a big impression on me.

Several years later I was in college and while my semi-serious relationship with God had continued I certainly had given no thought to a ministerial future. Like most students, I did not take the school's chapel requirement seriously. The auditorium where these chapel services were held was on the second floor of the building that I was responsible for cleaning so I had open access to the building. Late one night I put an alarm clock down in one of the organ pipes. The alarm was set to go off during the chapel period the next day and it produced the desired results. The president of the college was speaking in the chapel when the loud clanging began. It was noisy enough that it was not possible for him to continue whatever he was saying and the audience was finally dismissed.

The investigation that followed determined that the organ had malfunctioned and caused the racket in the pipe. I removed the alarm clock later that day and felt pleased to have committed the perfect crime. It did not occur to me that I might have been interfering with someone's religious devotion. If I had thought that requirement had much meaning I might have reconsidered my actions. However when I reflect on the poor quality of those chapel services I can't believe they would have inspired devotion in anyone.

From the hundreds of chapel services I was required to attend while in college I remember the message of only one. The speaker was none other than the son and namesake of the Dr. Currie who had put his hand on my head when I was a boy. Tom Currie II was a tall, lanky young man who to me resembled Abe Lincoln. That day he read and spoke about what I now know was the tenth chapter of the Book of Acts from the New Testament. That is the passage where the apostle Peter has the dream about a sheet being let down from heaven. It contained snakes and birds that were not appropriate for a devout Jew to eat. In spite of the religious law against eating such food, Peter received instructions from God that he could eat the unclean food. That experience was the beginning of Peter's understanding that the Good News of Jesus Christ is to show God's love for all people, not just the Jews.

Through the years I had trained myself not to listen to preachers' sermons so I may have missed most of the central message of the sermon that day but what did impress me was that this preacher used language that people could understand. When he talked about the dream with the food he used the words, "Barbequed pork ribs, hamburgers, and french fries." It was revolutionary for me to learn that a minister could speak in an understandable language. The thought that a preacher could be a real person was a new idea for me.

Several years later as I was wondering if I was really meant for the ministry I visited a class at Austin seminary. David Currie, a successful pastor of a Presbyterian church in Corpus Christi, Texas was to be the guest lecturer. David was another son of Dr. Thomas Currie. He was to speak on how a pastor plans his day. He began his lecture by describing the way he started most workdays. "After I shower, dress and have my morning prayers, I walk down to the church a few blocks from our house," he began. "Along the way to the church I stop by the drugstore and buy a newspaper and a cigar. When I arrive at my office I put my feet up on the desk, light the cigar and read the newspaper until the telephone rings. It is usually a call from a church member or someone else in need," he continued. "Then I fold up the newspaper, put out the cigar, and head for my car to go see someone who thinks I may be of help. That is how I plan my workdays," he concluded.

While I believe that part of what he described might have been a spoof, what was important to me was that if the primary role of a minister was to reach out to people in need I might be interested. David did not mention the one hundred other expectations placed on ministers but in his casual style he made his central point about the goal of being a minister, and that message impressed me.

Some years earlier Stuart Currie, who was yet another of the Currie brothers, married my cousin Sara. They had come to Itasca to visit Sara's parents, my Aunt Janie and Uncle Sidney Files. Stuart was a Presbyterian minister and had a reputation as a scholar. The word was that he sat around reading books all day.

My father went to visit his niece and her new husband when they paid that visit to Itasca. While he was there he noticed that the tires on their car were threadbare, and took the car to a garage to have a new set of tires installed. He said that he knew that a husband who sat around reading books all day was not going to notice worn out tires and he did not want his niece injured in an automobile accident caused by a blown out tire.

That was another part of my education about the ministry. A minister could be a scholar. I did not want to be a scholar but that a minister could be one was a new idea to me. The Currie family single-handedly fostered my interest in the ministry. Later another member of that family, Betty, helped me understand much of what I know about Christian Education.

Despite their influence I do not blame the Curries for my decision to enter the ministry. I can't say what precise combination of Itasca, my family, the church, my education or the Curie family played in my decision. It just seemed like what I was supposed to do. When I told my father my plans for the future his first question was, "If God wanted you to be a minister, why did He give you a voice like that?" It was hardly the support I had hoped for but I was off to seminary for training.

SOUTHERN LIVING

I had fully intended to spend the rest of my life in Texas. As I was finishing up my college days it occurred to me that choosing to attend a seminary outside of my home state might be interesting. So I enrolled in Union Seminary in Richmond, Virginia. I have sometimes said that decision ruined my life. It would probably be more accurate to say that the decision changed my life. Since I left for seminary training I have only lived in Texas a few years. That was not my plan. I thought I'd be right back in Texas for the rest of my life after I finished in Richmond.

Seminary days were spiritually, emotionally and mentally challenging for me. I experienced severe culture shock. People in Virginia spoke in such a strange way. They made the word "about" sounds like "a boot". They seemed to me to be into ancestral worship. They often asked newcomers, "And tell me, my dear, who was your grandfather?" How would I know? He was dead before I was born. When they talked about "The War," they did not mean the recently completed World War II. The Confederacy was still alive and well as witnessed by the statues on Monument Boulevard in Richmond. My history courses in Texas had called The Civil War "that war that South Carolina got us into." We were also told that our hero Sam Houston, as Governor of Texas, was in the basement of the Texas Capitol with tears in his eyes as the Legislature upstairs was impeaching him. He had refused to agree with Texas' withdrawal from the Union to join the Confederacy. I do not know if it was true but it is a good story and I believed that the Civil War was not an important part of my Texas heritage.

The academic level of the seminary was also a challenge for me compared to my high school and college days. I began to lose my contempt for academics. The things being taught were things I wanted to know. For the first time it began to dawn on me that the object of school was not just to do well on tests but was to learn. Seminary was also a time of spiritual and emotional testing. My Christian faith was challenged in a new way. I was clear about my relationship with God whom I had known since childhood. But it was a fairly naïve, unchallenged, simplistic faith. Seminary put some knowledge and muscle in my spiritual life and my relationship with the Divine. God and I had some pretty serious conversations about whether or not I was preparing myself properly to be a minister.

I had a scholarship for seminary that required me to work a certain number of hours a week. I was assigned a job in the library, and my first assignment was to dust and straighten the books on the shelves in the basement. I hated it. Dusting an endless row of books in a dark basement was a far cry from horseback riding in the sunshine on the north Texas plains.

One day the seminary librarian, Dr. Brim, called me into his office. He was a wonderful old man but I feared that I was about to be fired for my lack of book dusting skills. Instead he had a wonderful surprise for me. I think he sensed that I was going stir crazy. He explained to me that the seminary had bought a big house a few blocks away to be used for student housing. There were bookcases in the living room of this old mansion filled with books that Dr. Brim wanted brought to the library for sorting. His project for me was to drive his car to the house and bring the books back to the library. I felt like I had been given a temporary pardon from prison. I had not driven a car in weeks and to be out of the library basement felt like freedom. It was not the Texas plains but it was a few precious minutes outdoors.

With the car loaded with empty boxes, I drove the long way to the house enjoying the fall sunshine. I took boxes into the house and started loading the books. A woman came in and wanted to know what I was doing. I quickly told her that Dr. Brim had sent me to come get these books. I was not very friendly because I was eager to get back to work and do my job promptly and properly. I was hoping that I could prove myself worthy of other tasks outside of the dark library basement.

The woman left and as I finished packing the books and taking them to the car a man arrived. I knew him. He was Fred Stair, vice president of the Seminary. I had met him during our orientation on the first day. With a frown he asked what I was doing. I quickly explained that Dr. Brim had asked me to bring these books to the library. He left the room, saying that he needed to talk to Dr. Brim. I could hear him using the telephone in the next room.

He finished his call and returned greatly amused. I was embarrassed to learn that instead of going to the house that the seminary had purchased for student housing I had mistakenly gone to the vice president's home. Without knocking I had entered, packed his books, and put them in Dr. Brim's car. After I brought the books back in from the car, returned them to the shelves, apologized to the vice president and his wife for my intrusion into their home, I made my way to the appropriate house and completed my task there. I had failed my first outside job.

Early that fall I preached my first sermon. The experience was a mistake in more ways then one. It was 1949 and there had been a movement in the United States to develop some good will between Japan and the United States after the bitter years of World War II. One of the projects was the creation of a university as a gift to Japan from Christians in the United States. Many Presbyterian youth groups became involved in this project to establish the university. Seminary students were encouraged to help this movement and I was asked to go to Newport News, Virginia to speak to a youth group about the project. Excited about the opportunity I agreed to go.

On a chilly autumn day I caught the Greyhound Bus from Richmond to Newport News. I asked at the bus station for directions to the church and walked several blocks in the drizzling rain. When I arrived at the church it was locked and no one was there. I huddled out of the wind near the front door for almost an hour. I thought that the meeting was at 6 p.m. and wondered where everyone was.

Finally a man arrived who introduced himself as the pastor of the church. I explained what I was doing there and he told me he had not heard anything about a youth meeting that evening. He invited me into his office and made some telephone calls. No one else had heard about the meeting either.

Then with a bright smile on his face he said, "I have a wonderful idea. I feel like I am coming down with the flu and do not feel like preaching the sermon this evening. The service begins in half an hour. Since you are here would you be willing to preach for me?"

One of those moments of instant insanity overtook me and I agreed. I had not yet had a class in preaching at the seminary and had never prepared a sermon. It was then twenty minutes before the service was to begin and the pastor gave me a few minutes to collect my thoughts while he turned on the lights in the sanctuary.

My mind was a total blank when I was left alone in that room, and nothing had entered it by the time the minister returned. He handed me a printed order of worship for the evening service, and I absently put it in my coat pocket. Then opening a small closet, he pulled out a long black pulpit gown, and I stood there while he put it on me. He was a big tall man well over six feet in height. I was at least six inches shorter. The long robe made a puddle around my feet and my hands were nowhere near the ends of the long sleeves. He then led me to a door at the side of his office and opened it. Inside the door was the sanctuary of the church and we were standing at the side of the chancel. A little nudge in the small of my back and I stepped forward. It was then with horror that I realized he had closed the door behind me without coming in. He had gone home to nurse his flu leaving me alone to conduct the service.

I looked out at the congregation and they stared back. I walked over and sat down in one of the pulpit chairs as the organist concluded the prelude. She looked over at me and nodded her head. Obediently I walked up to the pulpit and looked into the faces of an expectant congregation. At that moment I realized that the bulletin with the order of worship was in my suit pocket inside the pulpit gown. With difficulty I managed to get my hands out of the long sleeves, unbutton part of the front of the robe and reach the inside pocket of my suit coat. I gave the folded paper a quick pull and out it came. So did my package of cigarettes. They spilled on the floor next to the pulpit. I looked at them and had to make a quick decision. Was it better to bend over and pick them up or to leave them on the floor? I left the cigarettes on the floor while the congregation watched with a mixture of amusement and disdain.

Now I had the order of service and we began the service. We managed through a hymn or two and a prayer without incident. Next came the Scripture reading. I had not chosen a reading but thought that I would go with something familiar such as John 3:16, "God so loved the world that He gave his only son..." I approached the big pulpit Bible and opened it knowing that the New Testament was about two-thirds from the beginning of the book. I was not a great Biblical scholar but I was familiar with the Scripture.

As I opened the Bible a strange thing happened. In front of my eyes was a book of the Bible I had never heard of before, the book of Maccabees. A bit shaken I turned some pages to find other books unknown to me—Tobit and Baruch. I was sure I was losing my mind. I later learned in church history classes that while these were books commonly included in Roman Catholic Bibles they had not been incorporated by those churches coming out of the Protestant Reformation. That information was not available to me that evening so I had to believe that either this was one strange Presbyterian Church I was in or that my sanity had disappeared. Flustered by the unfamiliar bible I gave up on finding a Scripture reading, said a few words from the 23rd Psalm, and quickly sat down.

Finally the time came for the sermon. I stood and began to say every religious thought that I could dredge up from my mind and memory. After I had spoken for what seemed a long time to me I sat down. I looked at my watch. I had spoken for four and a half minutes.

We had the closing hymn, I said a benediction, and I walked out the side door of the chancel without speaking to anyone. I left the pulpit gown in the pastor's closet and went out the back door for the long cold walk to the bus station. It was then I wished that I had stopped early in the service to retrieve the cigarettes that now lay on the floor of the church beside the pulpit. The only good thing I could think of was that no one in the congregation that evening knew who I was and I was not even certain that the pastor had gotten my name. It was a long bus ride back to Richmond after my first sermon. My preaching career was not off to a good start.

My seminary days were challenging. I grew serious about my studies, had some great professors and made good friends. Mentally and spiritually I was making good progress. However my emotional life was a wreck.

Much of my stress was because I was several hundred miles from my college sweetheart, Lou Alice. She was still in Texas for a last year of college and graduation. Letters and telephone calls were inadequate substitutes for hugs and kisses. We had agreed to date other people during this time apart but I had tasted the champagne of real love and other relationships were like flat beer. The second year I was in seminary Lou Alice came to Richmond to enter graduate school and we were married the next summer. My emotional life improved greatly after she arrived.

Our wedding took place in Beaumont, Texas where Lou Alice's father was the district manager for the telephone company. That position gave him a place of some importance in the civic and social world of the Beaumont community. The wedding was to take place in the First Presbyterian church on the last day of August in 1951. I was working that summer some distance away but was able to go to Beaumont one weekend for two necessary assignments.

One appointment was for a premarital counseling session

scheduled with the pastor of the Presbyterian Church. It was worth less than nothing. In fact it caused a misunderstanding in our marriage. The pastor had counseled us to follow the advice from the Bible in Ephesians 4:26 that says, "Do not let the sun go down upon your wrath." Either the pastor misquoted the Scripture or we misunderstood him because we came away with different interpretations and understandings of the passage.

I understood the verse to mean that if you came to the end of the day and had an unresolved issue, it was time to drop the subject and get a good night's sleep. This was the "no wrath and good night's sleep" interpretation.

Lou Alice had a "no sleep with wrath" approach. Her understanding led her to believe that the proper approach was to keep grinding on a disputed issue until it was resolved. That meant that when we had a disagreement, I would curl up in the bed ready for a good night's sleep. She would find that inappropriate and insist that we work though the unresolved issue even if it took all night.

This was not the first time that Christians had disagreed on the interpretation of Scripture as proven by the hundreds of churches and denominations in Christendom today. In spite of this and other differences, we've managed to keep our union intact for well over half a century. While we still may have differences of opinion on some issues, we usually do manage to "keep the sun from going down on our wrath."

My second assignment that summer for the same busy weekend was to rent tuxedoes for the five men in the wedding party. At some point in my life I had probably seen a man in a tux but I was certainly no men's fashion expert. I found in the Yellow Pages a store that rented formal wear. The man in the rental shop explained that our wedding was at the same time as another big social event taking place in Beaumont. Rental tuxedoes were limited. He asked about the number and sizes needed for the wedding party and went to the back of the shop to look. After a long delay he returned with the good news that he did have five tuxedoes in the correct sizes. He assured me that they were a formal Italian style that would be appropriate. I paid him and felt satisfied that I had completed my weekend assignments.

The day before the wedding I picked up the suits. When I went by Lou Alice's house her mother asked to see them. I brought one in from the car and slipped on the jacket. I kept trying to pull down the sleeves. They seemed a bit short and tended to balloon out around the elbow. The bottom of the jacket barely reached my waist. At that moment I remembered seeing similar jackets on waiters in Italian restaurants. After only a moment Lou Alice's mother said those three awful words, "That won't do".

I returned to the rental shop and was told that all of their tuxes had been rented. They let me use the telephone to call other shops but I couldn't find any that were available. I felt as if it were the end of the world—or at least surely the end of my marriage before it even began. In my despair I went to visit my parents who had driven to Beaumont for the wedding. They were staying with my father's cousin Richard. He and my father had joined the Marine Corps together and fought in Europe in World War I. I poured out my story of failure and after a few moments Richard said, "Bring your best man and groomsmen and meet me at the laundry at two o'clock this afternoon." It was then that I learned that he and a partner operated the largest dry cleaning shop and laundry in Beaumont.

We met him at the laundry at two o'clock and he took us

to the back of the building where we entered a huge refrigerated room. In that room were racks and racks of clothing that had been stored by customers for the summer to avoid the moths. Richard went through those racks and found tuxedos the right sizes for each of us.

Before we left he gave us a stern lecture about what would happen to us if we did not take good care of this borrowed clothing. The lecture was sprinkled with language that he must have learned in the Marine Corps and had been practicing for years. The social elite of Beaumont was unknowingly providing formal attire for the wedding and the marriage was saved. I was incredibly grateful to Richard and we took excellent care of the clothes.

The Wedding

Our honeymoon was the fourteen hundred mile drive from Texas to Virginia. We had just a few days to cover the distance and that was before the days of the Interstate Highway System. I knew it would be a long trip so I had properly prepared. The first morning as we were driving across Louisiana, Lou Alice mentioned that she would like to visit a ladies' room. I nodded and knowingly drove a few miles until I saw a dirt road turning off of the highway through a field of sugar cane. I drove up the road a few hundred yards, stopped the car and opened the glove compartment. It was with a smug sense of pride that I handed a brand new roll of toilet paper to my bride.

At that moment I began my lifelong education in Husband 101. I learned that when Lou Alice said she wanted to visit the ladies' room she meant a shining clean rest room in a nice service station that I should find almost immediately. I have still not graduated from that Husband's Course but I learned enough that day to get back on the road and find her a ladies' room.

In Richmond we moved into a small two-room basement apartment not far from the seminary. Our living room had a bachelor's kitchen with a little sink, a two-burner stove and a small refrigerator built into the wall. Soon after we moved in I noticed that there were tooth marks appearing on the butter and cheese in our refrigerator. Lou Alice was a very well mannered person and it struck me as rather strange that she would bite off of food like that but I didn't want to say anything. I knew that marriage demanded compromise and some adjustments so I avoided mentioning her peculiar habit.

I admit I was relieved one day when I opened the refrigerator and saw a cute little mouse eating the cheese. He had gnawed a hole around the condenser pipe and was coming in through the back of the refrigerator. He could eat our leftovers and then retire for the evening to his home between the walls. What an ideal situation for a mouse but I couldn't let him freeload off of us anymore.

I set a mousetrap in the refrigerator and it wasn't long until it caught him. However, when I set the trap I had forgotten that I was going to be away for a few days on a trip. I also never guessed that Lou Alice would not be willing to remove a dead mouse. She had opened the refrigerator door once, seen the dead mouse and promptly closed the door. She ate out while I was gone and ruined our whole month's grocery budget.

I still had some things to learn about living with a woman, but every little bit I learned helped me. I learned two important things about Lou Alice from this event. She did not periodically gnaw on food straight out of the refrigerator, and she would rather decimate our grocery budget than touch a dead mouse. After all, since it was my fault for putting the mousetrap in the refrigerator when I wasn't going to be home, what could she do but eat out? Our love and marriage prevailed.

As we approached the end of my seminary work we began to make plans for the future. We had both expressed an interest in overseas missionary service. Lou Alice had said, "Why would we want to work in the United States where there are plenty of churches and where you end up begging people to become involved? Why not go overseas where people do not have the same opportunity to know of God's love and who are eager to hear and to help?" That thought resonated with me. We applied and were accepted by the Presbyterian Church for overseas service in what was then the Belgian Congo in West Africa.

We still had to meet a few requirements. First I had to graduate from seminary and be ordained. There was also a requirement that ministers have a year of pastoral experience prior to overseas service.

The ordination process was conducted in the large First Presbyterian Church in Houston, Texas before a gathering of several hundred Presbyterian ministers and elders. My first assignment was to preach before that assembly in this imposing sanctuary. Following was a series of oral examinations administered in front of the audience. The examiners included the President, the Dean, a Professor and the Chairman of the Board of the Austin Presbyterian Theological Seminary. What made this challenging was that as a native Texan I had been disloyal enough to go off to a foreign seminary in Virginia rather than to attend my own seminary in Texas.

I have always believed that the exam was particularly grueling for me so that the leaders of the Texas seminary could demonstrate that my education at a Virginia seminary was inferior. They may have been correct, but the real deficiency demonstrated by my exam was my lack of academic diligence, and not the credibility of the out-of-state institution. Neither was the process helped for me by the fact that one of my old college friends stood in the balcony of the church making faces at me and performing obscene gestures. I was the only one who could see him. He later claimed that he was there to help settle my nerves. I didn't murder him but I confess it crossed my mind that day. With God's grace my examination for ordination was approved.

Another requirement to be met for overseas service was a minimum age of twenty-five. When I graduated from seminary, we were two years short of the age requirement. Two small churches in Texas agreed to call me as their pastor for one year. Then there was a one-year program in Belgium required for missionaries who were to be certified School Directors in their African colony. By spending a year as a pastor in Texas and a year in Europe we could meet the age requirement for service in Africa. With this plan we were anxiously ready to meet our new world.

THE ROAD TO AFRICA

On the way to Africa our trip first took us to Central Texas where I was to be the pastor of churches in Calvert and in Maysfield to fulfill the requirement for pastoral experience. We moved into the manse next door to the church in the little town of Calvert. Maysfield was a farming community fifteen miles away. The people in both congregations were generous and kind in accepting a green, inexperienced young preacher and his wife. I have often thought that those churches deserved a part of the tuition that I paid the seminary for my ministerial training.

I was discouraged after preaching my first sermon in Calvert. When I began preaching an elderly gentleman sitting on the right side of the sanctuary rather obviously removed a hearing aid from each of his ears. I took this as a sign that he was not interested in anything I was going to say. Another man sitting directly in front of the pulpit spent the whole time I was preaching shaking his head from side to side as if disapproving of each point as I made it. I later learned that the man with the hearing aids had been asked to remove them during the sermon because they had a tendency to produce unexpected loud squealing noises disrupting those around him. The man with the disapproving headshake had a neurological problem, and his gestures were involuntary. Since I had assumed the worst during the sermon, it was a tough way to begin my career as a preacher.

Lou Alice and I were the only young couple around and so when our first child was born, our son John had a host of honorary aunts and uncles among the church members. He was born twenty miles away in the nearest hospital in Marlin, Texas. Years earlier the town had been famous for some healing springs that bubbled out of the ground. Folks came from miles around to cure their ills in these mineral waters. A combination hospital and hotel had been built on the site of the springs. This unique building boasted a portable cloth screen that determined the line between the hospital and the hotel rooms. The screen could be moved back and forth to accommodate more or fewer hospital patients or hotel guests. I was never certain if our son was born in a hotel or a hospital.

To celebrate the birth of our son the congregation in Calvert gave us a beautiful blue satin comforter for the bed. The church members in Maysfield were also excited about his birth and gave us an identical satin comforter in green. As church members came by to pay their respects and to see the new baby we would keep an eye out our front window to see whether the visitors walking up the steps were from Calvert or Maysfield. We'd quickly check to ensure the appropriate comforter was on the bed.

My time in Calvert provided me with one of my early ecumenical experiences. The town was also home to a thriving Baptist church and I had come to know a number of the members. On Tuesday nights the Baptist men met for their Brotherhood meeting. After a quick devotional they moved to the significant part of the meeting—playing dominos. They invited me to join them, and as an old domino and forty-two player with few other recreational opportunities, I was delighted. I became good friends with our Baptist neighbors. When a new pastor came to their church he did not think that it was appropriate for a non-immersed Presbyterian to be a part of their meetings.

This became an issue of significant controversy and some of the men threatened to leave and start another Baptist church. I had always heard that one of the reasons there are so many different Baptist churches is that every time there is a disagreement, some members just split and start another. We certainly had enough Baptist churches in our area, so I withdrew and quit going to the Baptist Brotherhood meetings. I did miss the domino games.

Being a new pastor brought about a change in my spiritual life. While I had primarily focused on my own Christian development and growth at the seminary I was now responsible for nurturing others' faith. I am not sure how well I performed this function. In some ways it seemed that I had been a rider on the faith bus who had been suddenly asked to take the wheel.

A few years ago I went through the files of my old sermons. As I read my early messages I noticed that they often repeated lectures from seminary or made reference to theological books. There was not much there to reflect my own faith and commitment. I threw those old sermons away and was reminded that my first year as a pastor was a great leaning experience for me, but probably of minimum benefit to the congregations. They were very gracious about it, and not too long ago, I met a woman whose baby I baptized while in Maysfield over fifty years ago. Recently she introduced me to her middle-aged son and he is a fine man. I believe that the baptism must have taken. God must have been watching me in those early days with the same nervousness parents feel when their teenager is learning to drive.

Part of our time during that first year out of seminary was spent preparing supplies for our time in Africa. We had been sent a long list of food and other necessities we would need for our three-year stay in the African bush well removed from shopping opportunities. We were to be in a remote area that was at least a day's drive by jeep over dirt roads to reach a town of any size. We could find some fruits, vegetables, beans and rice in the local outdoor market but we would need to order our other supplies from Europe and have them shipped to us.

We were not exactly experienced dieticians and housekeepers. How much powdered milk would we need for three years in the bush? We would have the same questions for salt, pepper, sugar, canned tomatoes, spinach, and vanilla flavoring and for dozens of other items. I calculated the toilet paper supply as a math problem. Lou Alice and I counted the number of sheets we used in a day. I added these numbers and divided the total into the number of sheets in a roll. That gave me the number of days a roll would last. I divided that number into 1,095, the number of days we would be in the Congo before returning to the U. S. on furlough. My math was correct but my formula was flawed. I did not calculate that before we returned to the U. S. we would have three children. Neither did the calculation take into account that our digestive tracts would react rather violently to some African microorganisms. These situations would necessitate the use of considerably more toilet paper than I had imagined.

While I under-estimated some of the supplies we would need I over-estimated others. I had heard the old adage that one bottle of Tabasco Sauce would last through the length of most marriages. I did not know that a bottle of lemon extract would last almost as long as Tabasco and I ordered a carton of twenty-four bottles—more than we could ever think about using. Since we did not have any other alcoholic beverages, and I noticed that lemon flavoring had a high alcohol content, I tried to make lemon extract cocktails for a New Year's celebration one year. After that it was years before I could eat a lemon pie.

We were also told to pack all of the clothes we would need for the next four years. Our son, John, was born that year and I remember walking into a department store, going to the children's department, and asking a clerk to help us find all of the shoes, socks, pants, shirts, pajamas, underwear and other clothing this three months old baby would need for the next four years. She was overwhelmed. We did not know that we would have a second child in Belgium where we spent a year preparing for Africa, or that our third son would be born while we were in Africa. With no department stores selling children's clothing available, the word, "hand-me-down" took on a whole new meaning.

Packing for Africa was a major project. We were told to put whatever we were shipping to Africa in fifty-five gallon steel drums. I bought the barrels from a bakery that had received them full of shortening. I spent hours scrubbing the inside of them to remove the grease. We then packed them with clothes, books, dishes, and other household and personal items.

After a year as a pastor in Texas we still had a detour on our road to Africa. We first spent a summer in an orientation program in Montreat, North Carolina, and then went by ship to Europe.

We were headed for the Belgian Congo, a colony of the Belgian government located in West Africa. A part of my assignment in the Congo was to assist with educational development. That required me to spend a year in the Colonial School in Brussels so that the government would certify me as a school director. I arrived in Belgium knowing no French for courses that would be taught in that language. The program required me to pass exams in several courses including Belgium and African history, geography, tropical medicine, pedagogy, and colonial regulations—all taught in French. Only one of the several diplomas I have earned through my studies now hangs on the wall of my office. That is my certificate from the Belgian Government. That diploma reminds me not of my language and academic skills but of a miracle and the power of prayer involved in receiving it.

My diploma was not the only reward we received that year. Lou Alice learned how to have a baby in French and our second son, Paul, was born in Brussels. After a long cold winter we finally boarded a ship for Africa and were on our way to fulfilling a dream.

We did learn that if you want to be a missionary you had better enjoy traveling. After two weeks onboard ship with a stop in the Canary Islands and Angola, we arrived at Matadi, the Congo seaport. We spent a day making a hazardous drive on unmarked dirt roads to the Capitol city of Leopoldville, now Kinshasa. From there we took a plane to the interior and then took a one-day's jeep ride through the bush to our remote station. We managed all of this travel with a one year old child and a baby.

We moved into a small one-bedroom house with cement floors and a corrugated metal roof. Wood was not a popular building material because it was a favorite meal of termites and other insects. Even our bathtub was made of cement. Our water was supplied from a barrel on the roof of the house. Each day a workman walked back and forth to the river several times. It was a half-mile trip each way. He carried back to our house two buckets of water swinging from a pole placed across his shoulders. He then climbed a ladder to the roof and poured the water into the barrel. In the late afternoon the workman built a wood fire under a coil of pipes at the side of the house. The pipes ran from the barrel on the roof to the coil and then on to our bathroom. If the fire was hot enough and you were quick enough, the process supplied warm water for a bath of a few inches in the cement tub. All of our drinking water had to be boiled and filtered. Our kitchen and wood stove was in a small lean-to built on the back of the house.

We had electricity for one hour each evening when there was fuel for the generator. We liked to use the time when there was power to listen to the BBC from London on the radio and be reminded that there was still a world out there. It took weeks for our mail to reach us. It made part of its slow trip by riverboat before it was delivered to us.

Do you know what an icy ball is? It is a jungle icemaker that consists of two cast-iron balls about the size of bowling balls with one slightly larger than the other. A metal pipe about four feet long connects the balls. To make the contraption work, the larger ball was placed in a hot wood fire and allowed to heat to a very high temperature. The heated ball was then placed in a tub of cool water. This change in temperature caused the smaller ball on the other end of the pipe to become cold. There was even a little four-cube ice tray. The cold ball was then put into a big, insulated wooden box with a slot in the side to allow the pipe and larger ball to hang outside. It was indeed a primitive refrigerator but it provided us with a place to keep our food cool. We later graduated to a kerosene refrigerator.

Life in Africa was an overwhelming experience. We found the Africans to be a patient, warm, and friendly people. They welcomed us with enthusiasm and openness in spite of our limited language skills. While a few of the Africans knew some French, Tshiluba was the common language where we first lived. We immediately began studying Tshiluba. I had studied Spanish in high school, Greek in collage, Hebrew in seminary, French in Brussels and was now required to learn my fifth language in a few short years. God was not being an easy taskmaster.

The Tshiluba language spoken in Central Congo offered a special challenge. It is a tonal language. That means that each syllable of a word may be a different tone. For instance in a word the first tone may be high and the second tone may be low. If the tones are reversed the word will have a totally different meaning. The spelling for the words for heaven and nose is the same. However, when speaking the words, the tones for the two syllables are different. It was not unusual for new missionaries to begin the Lord's Prayer, not with the usual "Our Father who art in heaven," but with the words, "Our Father who art in the nose." The Africans were good-natured about our mistakes.

Verbs, objects and adjectives are adjusted to use the prefix of the subject of the sentence. For instance the word in Tshiluba for cloth is **tshi**lamba. The word for clothes is **bi**lamba. Watch how the other words use the prefixes of **tshi** and **bi**.

This cloth is pretty. **Tshi**lamba e**tshi** **tshi**de **tshi**mpe.

or

These clothes are pretty. **Bi**lamba e**bi** **bi**di **bi**mpe.

The interesting use of different tones and the repeated use of the subject's prefix give the language a lyrical sound with wonderful sense of rhyme.

Adapting to an African culture brought some surprises. One afternoon, a day or two after we had moved into our small house, it began to rain. I happened to look out of the window and was startled to see four nude women standing at the corner of our house engaged in a vigorous dance. I was puzzled by this strange sight and later learned that the women were simply taking a shower under the water that was running off of the gutter from our roof. It made good sense. It was not safe to bathe in the river because of the crocodiles. The roof of the grass and stick huts in which the women lived did not produce a flow of water from the rain like the gutter on our metal roof. In addition, African modesty held a very different view of when and where nudity was acceptable. I had a lot to learn.

One of the most valuable lessons I learned was not about nudity but about the spiritual life. The Africans I knew had a heritage of animism and so understood a world where rocks, trees, and all living things have a spiritual life or dimension. This was a helpful addition to my materialistic view of physical objects. This spiritual view of the world enhanced my ability to know and understand the presence of God. The line between the physical and the spiritual was not as clear as I had thought. I was helped to grasp a sense of the nearness of God that my materialistic view of the world did not provide. I knew the words that "God is everywhere," but I had imagined a fairly firm wall existing between the physical world and the spiritual one. In good moments I can now almost see over that wall.

Another gift the Africans gave me was a new understanding of the church. When we lived in Africa fifty years ago the most important thing in a person's life was his or her tribe. The tribe was like a large family and it inspired a strong sense of loyalty. It gave that person an identity. As Africans became Christians and members of a church, they saw the church as a new tribe.

They did not lose their membership in the family tribe. Instead they brought that same sense of loyalty and new identity into the New Tribe of Jesus Christ—the church. That looked to me much more like the early New Testament church than some of the American ones that seem more like social clubs.

Another experience gave me a new appreciation for the Bible. Not long after we arrived in the Congo one of the veteran missionaries took me on a trip into the deep interior. We spent the night in a village and that evening there was a special ceremony. During the event one of the men stood near a large campfire and recited a long story. I knew little of the language but later my missionary friend explained to me the man speaking was the tribal historian. He was telling the history of the tribe—naming the chiefs and the places the tribe had lived. He was reciting the oral history of the tribe.

What impressed me about that evening ceremony was that it gave new meaning to what my Bible professors had told us about the Bible. They had explained that many parts of the Old Testament, before being put into writing, had been passed down through generations as oral tradition. In the same way the African speaking that night was preserving the history of his tribe in a situation where the written language was not yet known. I was seeing before my eyes what the words "oral tradition" really meant.

The vitality of the Christian faith expressed in the lives and worship of my African friends was an inspiration to me. Instead of the dull, predictable, formal Presbyterian worship I had become accustomed to, African worship was lively with enthusiastic singing, swaying, and dancing. The preaching was vigorous and the congregation frequently participated. The minister would begin a Scripture verse and the congregation would complete it. The preacher would ask a rhetorical question and a hardy response from the congregation would follow. The sermon was no time or place for a brief nap.

The faith commitment of many of the Africans was striking. Many were generous in giving to the church. One member of our congregation was a very old widow who lived in a small hut. She owned one old hen and the eggs from the hen were her primary means of support. Yet almost every Sunday that woman brought one egg and solemnly put that one seventh of her weekly income into the offering plate.

Early in the twentieth century Protestants agreed to geographically divide the world and to assign particular areas to denominations for their "foreign mission work." One of the areas given to our Presbyterian church was a part of the central interior of the Belgian Congo. Later, there was an explosion of population growth nearer the coast in and around the capital city of Leopoldville. The American and British Baptist churches that had been assigned that area were overwhelmed by the growth, and invited the Presbyterians to come join in the efforts there.

After a year at our remote outpost, Lou Alice and I were one of the two couples assigned to begin the Presbyterian work in Leopoldville. It was an exciting place to be but it did mean more linguistic punishment for me. I had to learn Lingala, yet another new language. God must have smiled at that.

I had two assignments in the Congo after we moved to the capital city. One task was to establish primary schools. The Belgium government was trying to institute a system of elementary education. The State provided support for teachers, buildings and books. With the certificate I had earned in Belgium I was qualified to be a director of this program.

Parents were eager for their children to be in school and on enrollment day there was always a huge crowd. Only children six years of age or older could be enrolled. Since there were no birth certificates, some parents would try to enroll younger children. How could we tell the difference in a five year old and a six-year-old child? A pediatric physician who studied the physical development of children solved the problem. When a child places his or her hand directly over the top of his or her head at the age of six, the fingers will normally just reach the top of the ear on the other side. This became the test for school enrollment. I can still see mothers in line with small children pulling the child's arm, trying to make the arm long enough to reach the far ear.

The government, who carefully monitored the program, sent inspectors to evaluate the teacher's daily lesson plans. For the early grades we had no books, so their lessons were taught from a blackboard. Pupils sat on benches made from split logs in open-air classrooms. Each student had a small slate and a stylus since pencils and paper were not available. It was a primitive start but learning did take place.

My second assignment was to serve as an evangelist. An African evangelist and I began a church in a new housing development in the city. I obtained some metal roofing and other materials from a Greek merchant who was tearing down an old building. With the help of some members of the congregation we constructed a large open-air structure that would seat several hundred people. Open backed benches provided seating, and what we lacked in physical accommodations was made up for by the enthusiasm and dedication of the worshipers. That congregation continued to grow, and over the years with other Presbyterian churches in the area reached out into the surrounding area and planted new churches. The church we started there recently celebrated its 50th year as The Presbyterian Church of Kinshasa and now has thousands of members.

Children in Front of Church

As the church was growing so was our family. Our third son, Sam, was born while we lived in Kinshasa. The doctor on duty at the hospital in Kinshasa was from Germany. He did not speak English and his limited use of French included some of his native German words. In a four-year period Lou Alice had given birth to three children on three different continents in three different languages. A few years later when she was pregnant again we lived in Texas. I offered to take her to South America for a birth in Spanish, a fourth language on a fourth continent. She declined.

After one year in Europe and three years in Africa the time came for us to return to the United States for a furlough. We were four years older, the parents of three children, had studied three languages, and had lived in very different cultures. We had reluctantly and sometimes painfully become grownups.

HOME AGAIN WITH DETOURS

We left Africa in the mid spring of 1956 for a return to the United States after being gone for almost four years. We thought it would be fun to stop over in Rome, Venice, Paris, and London for a few days' vacation on the way home. What were we thinking? Our oldest child, John, was barely four years old, Paul was three, and Sam was one. It was not much of a vacation with three small children, one still in diapers in the days before diapers were disposable.

We arrived in Rome in early April. The weather was cool, and according to Italian custom, the heat in the hotel had been turned off the first of April. Three years in the tropics had thinned our blood. We were freezing. I went down to the see the manager of the hotel and explained our predicament hoping that he could supply some heat to our room. He pleasantly agreed to help us. I returned to the room and announced that my errand had been successful. Help was on the way! A few minutes later there was a knock on the door. I expected a person with a space heater. Instead there was a waiter with five glasses of brandy. I was not certain if the brandy was to warm our bodies or to make us forget about being cold. We had read a few books on childcare, and we were fairly certain that brandy was not on the recommended diet for children age four and under. We continued our vacation through Italy, France, and England before returning home.

Europe was not a very child-friendly place in those days, but when we returned to Texas some days later we received a warm welcome from grandparents who were eager to see these grandsons, two of whom had been born overseas and that they had not seen. We settled into a duplex in Austin, Texas, where we were expected to spend a year on furlough. We had been there only a few weeks when we were asked to move to Nashville, Tennessee, the location of the offices of the Presbyterian Mission Board where I would be working as part of the office staff.

After moving to Nashville and settling into a small rented house, one of my first assignments was to go to a large Presbyterian Men's Convention held in Miami. I was to set up and manage a display demonstrating the church's overseas work. I remember two things about those meetings. First, Billy Graham was one of the speakers. The other thing was that at the end of the meeting when I was packing up the display, I began to have some numbness in my right arm and hand.

After returning to Nashville, the problem in my hand and arm continued. Lou Alice noticed an article in the newspaper that pointed out that sleeping with a hand and arm over the head could cause numbness in that area the next day. The cure was to sew the pajama sleeve to the pajama pants so that the arm could not be raised during the night. It seemed worth a try. It made getting into pajamas a bit awkward, and it limited me to using one hand. Little did I know that I would eventually learn a lot more about using only one hand.

The home remedy did not work and the problem worsened. The doctors at Vanderbilt Hospital thought that the problem must have been related to malaria or some exotic African disease and ordered extensive tests. They sent me to Barnes Hospital in St. Louis and Johns Hopkins in Baltimore for further testing that also produced no conclusions. At one time they did some psychological testing, and one of the doctors was intrigued with an idea that perhaps seeing Billy Graham just before the onset of these problems might have been significant. While in seminary I had gone down front during the alter call at one of his revival services and several years later we lived across the street from him in Montreat, North Carolina, but never for a minute did I imagined that Billy Graham was in some way responsible for my physical difficulties.

My illness became more severe and so did the procedures. Before one of them a nurse shaved my head and gave the hair to Lou Alice saying, "If he doesn't make it, the undertakers can use this to make him look real natural." There was nothing natural about the procedure. Two holes of about half an inch in diameter were drilled in my head to allow further examination. I was sedated but not anaesthetized for this procedure, and it was extremely painful and unpleasant.

Even more unpleasant surprises were in store. For a while I lost the ability to recognize many simple words in print, and equally frightening I would confuse words in my speech. Complete paralysis set in on the right side of my body and slowly covered the left side. With no diagnosis of the problem, after two months I was sent home from the hospital. Along with three small children to care for Lou Alice now had an incapacitated husband who could not walk, sit up, feed himself or dress himself. Without a whimper, this determined woman took over all responsibility for our family.

There was a time when the paralysis made it impossible for me to use either of my hands. Since some documents needed my signature, I learned to sign my name and write a bit by holding a pencil in my mouth. Over the months some of the paralysis began to recede and with the help of a physical therapist I learned to walk.

The ordeal also left me an emotional wreck. I remember one afternoon after I had learned to walk, Lou Alice drove me to the barbershop. She let me out of the car and I went in. The barber greeted me and I immediately burst into tears. I walked back outside and sat on the curb of the street sobbing until Lou Alice returned.

Over a two-year period I regained the use of most of my body except for the right arm and hand. They remained paralyzed for over five years. The disease remained undiagnosed and some people attributed my recovery to my prayers. I knew better. It was much more likely that it was Lou Alice's prayers and determination.

It was during that period of time that Plymouth designed an automobile with an automatic transmission that operated by pushing buttons on the left side of the dashboard. It was wonderful for me because it had been almost impossible for me to manage shifting gears on the right side of the steering wheel with only the use of my left arm. I displayed my gratitude by driving Plymouths for a number of years, even after regaining most of the use of my right arm and hand.

I remember a man seriously saying how wonderful it was that God had led the Plymouth people to design the push-button transmission controls, and had led them to put the control box on the left side so that I could reach it. It never occurred to me to blame God for my sickness and handicap. I am also reluctant to believe that God directed a Plymouth car designer to come up with this arrangement in 1955 just so I could continue to drive.

Neither did I give much credence to a message a woman brought to me one day. With great earnestness she looked me in the eye and said, "God has made you sick because there is a lesson you need to learn, and you will not get well until you learn it." I did learn a lot of things. I learned that with only one hand it is difficult to tie your shoes, open a door that requires turning a key and doorknob simultaneously, cut meat on a dinner plate or give your wife or child a big bear hug. Only one hand and arm will not do any of these things properly.

With all my being I believe that God created and is in charge of this world. I also have faith that God has a plan and remains in ultimate control. But how, when, and where this all works in human history I do not know, and am suspicious of those who claim to know those detailed answers. During those dark days I saw God's care for me in the persistent prayers, love, and care Lou Alice and others gave me. For me faith is about trust and love rather than about knowledge of how, when, and where God works.

As I was recovering from this no-name disease, my mother came from Texas to Nashville to visit. She was concerned about my health and strangely also began to develop numbness in her hand and arm. After she returned home her condition became even more serious and she was hospitalized.

After several months I was able to return to the office for a few hours a day, but my mother's health continued to deteriorate. One morning I received a telephone call saying that I should come to Texas immediately if I wanted to see my mother alive. I was on the next airplane from Nashville to Dallas. It is with some embarrassment that I realize now that I had left Lou Alice to come to Texas later in the day with our three small children. For that I could have been charged with spousal abuse.

My aunt and uncle met me at the Dallas airport for the hour's trip to Itasca. On the drive my aunt told me how glad my mother would be to see me. She went on to explain what a remarkable recovery mother had made, and that she, my aunt, had visited with my mother in the grocery store just that morning. I found the story incredible but desperately wanted to believe it. When we arrived in Itasca and I saw the faces of my father and sister it was clear that the message was untrue. My aunt was suffering from dementia, and my uncle had not bothered to tell me. My mother had died earlier in the day.

The following morning I drove to the county seat of Hillsboro to the hospital where my mother had died. I went in to pick up her clothes and personal belongings. As I was leaving the room I met a bright looking young man in the hall who introduced himself as a doctor from Waco. He asked if I was Mrs. Coffin's son. When I said that I was, he explained that he was a psychiatrist who had been called in on the case. He said that he had read my mother's files, had identified the problem, and believed that he could have her in good health in short order. He had assumed that she had a psychosomatic problem that some counseling would relieve. I had to inform him that she had died the day before from an aneurysm that had ruptured near the brain.

My aunt's dementia and the misinformed psychiatrist were severe tests for my emotions that were already weakened by my illness. My father had a way of bringing me back to reality. He sent my sister and me to make the funeral arrangements. The furniture store in our town had a couple of small rooms in the back where embalmment took place and caskets were sold. Jane and I met with Fred, the store manager, selected a nice, modest-priced casket, and made other arrangements for the funeral and burial. We returned home to tell Daddy about the plans we had made.

His first question was, "How much will it cost?" We told him that the total price was $650. "Six hundred and fifty dollars!" he exclaimed. "You go tell Fred that if he can't do it for three hundred dollars I'll hire a couple of hands and go do it myself."

While it sounded crude, my sister and I recognized that our father was dealing with his grief by reverting to his basic need to trade for a good deal even on a matter of such sensitivity. It did help me regain some sense of reality after the bizarre encounters with my aunt and the psychiatrist.

We went back and explained the situation to Fred. He charged $300 for the casket, funeral and burial. When my father died a few years later Fred told us he knew exactly what kind of funeral Daddy would want and that the charge was $300.

It was clear that my medical condition would not allow us to continue our career in Africa. My contract with the Overseas Mission Board in Nashville was coming to a close. My father was in poor health and we wanted to be close enough to keep an eye on him. So we moved back to Texas.

My father's last years were not kind to him. My mother, who had cared for him in his bad health, had died. After that it was a contest each day to see if his heart, his lungs, or his disposition would be in the worst shape. He lived alone, by his choice, and Tom, now an old man who had worked for the family for years. came in each day to cook, do light housekeeping, and run necessary errands. A time came when Daddy ultimately needed to be in a hospital, but he was against it. The pleas of his doctor and family eventually persuaded him, and he agreed to enter the Veterans Hospital in Temple, Texas. He did not know much about the quality of medical care at the Veterans Hospital but he liked the price. My father was not greedy but he was "close with a dollar" as they said in our town. He chose the Veterans Hospital on the basis of the price—it was free.

The night before he was admitted to the hospital I drove the hundred miles from our home in Austin to spend the night with him. He was a bit anxious the next morning as we drove the seventy-five miles to the Veterans Hospital, but he was a good sport about it. We went first to the admitting office, an encounter that I did not anticipate with pleasure. My experience with hospital admission procedures was that the process took unusual patience—a quality my father had never possessed. Although he made some rather pointed suggestions about how he thought their procedures could be improved, he managed the process better than I expected.

Next we went down a long hall to a room where clothes and supplies were issued to patients. He was given military pajamas, a bathrobe, slippers, razor, toothbrush, and everything else needed for a hospital stay.

My father then went behind a curtain to change his clothes. An orderly handed me my father's jacket, shirt, pants, and boots. I took the clothes out to our car in the parking lot. When I returned I heard the orderly saying to him, "Mr. Coffin, you may get by with the hat, but I don't think they are going to let you keep the pistol." My father was certainly not a gangster. He was in the banking and ranching business. But he frequently carried a handgun and always slept with one. The pistol had prevented at least two bank robberies, killed dozens of snakes on the ranch and had been his constant companion since his early days in the military and in the untamed oil fields.

My father came out from behind the curtain wearing his Stetson hat, a bathrobe and slippers. There was a bulge in the pocket of the bathrobe just the size of a thirty-eight-caliber revolver. We took the elevator up to the floor where he had been assigned to a large ward with fifty or sixty beds. We were immediately very popular with the staff because the orderly had reported my father's weapon. The floor nurse, the head nurse, the resident physician, the chaplain, the psychiatrist, and the hospital administrator gathered around us. A couple of security guards also appeared. Several dozen patients formed a half circle around my father's bed, happy to have some diversion from dreary life on the ward.

The discussion reached its peak when the administrator, a small man with dark eyes too close together and a voice as sharp as the north wind, said to the psychiatrist, "See, I told you he was crazy."

My father replied in a well-modulated tone, "It's funny that I don't feel crazy. I believe that we just have a conflict of rules here. You have a rule that I can't have my pistol. I have a rule that I can't sleep without it. If I were crazy, I would have given you the pistol and then I would have to stay here and break my rule. I kept my pistol so now I can leave."

Turning to me he said, "Get my hat, son." I handed him the Stetson off of the bedside table. He put it on his head and with his hand in the pocket with the pistol we made our way to the elevator and then out to the car.

As we drove out of the parking lot and then back to the highway there was a long silence. Then he said resolutely, "Sometimes you just have to know what you believe and hang on to it." A few months later my Father died in his bed at home where he wanted to be. I was glad that we had moved to Texas to be near him.

Daddy In His Hat

I had become the pastor of a small church on the west side of Austin, Texas. The church had grown out of a mission Sunday school in the hills across the Colorado River from Austin where the primary income for much of the population had traditionally come from cutting cedar trees to be used for fence posts. Recently this had become a popular place for university professors and other professionals to build homes secluded in the woods. The small congregation included educated university professors, high-income professionals, low-income workers and some families on welfare. There was a wonderful mix of people in the congregation, and they graciously accepted a preacher recovering from a mysterious disease. One who could not even shake hands with church members at the end of the Sunday worship service because of his paralyzed right arm.

One of the advantages of serving a church near Austin was that the Presbyterian seminary in that city offered students to help in local churches so that they could gain some experience. However there were times when those students brought some headaches.

One of the students sent to help us was a young woman who wanted to try some new approaches. Her assignment at the church was to work with the junior high students. The students liked her because she enjoyed developing non-traditional plans and young teenagers are often drawn to the unconventional. Her creativity was challenged as we approached Christmas that year. She planned a special Christmas program, but the usual nativity scene was not good enough for her.

The youth group met at the church on Sunday evenings from 6:30 to 8:00. One Sunday evening about 8:30 my telephone began to ring. I was receiving calls from the parents of the junior high students who had arrived at home after the meeting at the church. The program the seminary student had prepared for them that evening intrigued the young people. Since it was the Christmas season, it was not surprising that the program was on the birth of Jesus. What was surprising was that as a part of the program the students had role-played the Virgin Birth.

I do not know what images come to your mind as you think about young teenagers role-playing the Virgin Birth, but the parents of these students were not at all pleased. Nor was I pleased with the time I had to spend trying to help this seminary student develop some common sense, and not engage in what in the South might be called "Po Taste."

That same year I had a young seminary student assigned to me. He was overly eager and wanted to learn everything immediately. Soon after this man began shadowing me, I was to hold a funeral for one of our church members. The man was a retired Army Major who was highly respected in the church and the community and it was important for him to be given a proper burial.

The seminary student pleaded with me to let him have a part in the service. I explained to him that this service was very important to the family and friends of the deceased. There would be a large gathering, and it was not a good time for him to practice participating in the service. He persisted and suggested that I let him put on a robe and sit at the front of the church with me but stay silent. He would simply follow me around during the service. I reluctantly agreed. The funeral service went well, and while it may have looked a bit strange he obediently followed me into the sanctuary, sat quietly during the service, and followed me out at the end.

He also came with me to the cemetery for the burial service. He behaved very well and stayed a foot or two behind me as I stood next to the grave. At one point during the graveside service, after the casket had been lowered into the grave, a military guard of soldiers nearby raised their rifles and fired a salute to the Major being buried. The loud noise from the rifles startled me and caused me to stumble a bit. When I realized that I was about to step into the open grave, I caught myself and jumped across to land safely on the other side. As I was collecting myself, I looked back over the grave and saw the seminary student making his jump to come stand next to me. He made it and stood there obediently for the rest of the service.

I never confessed to him that I had lost my balance, and that jumping over open graves was not a traditional part of a burial service. All these years later he may be following the practice he thought he learned from me that day. He may still be jumping over open graves.

While we lived in Austin, our fourth son, David, was born. My health had improved, the church had grown, and it was time for a new challenge. While we not able to return to our overseas mission service as we had originally planned, we were invited to return to the staff of the office of the Board of World Missions in Nashville.

TO NASHVILLE AND ATLANTA

The ten years we spent in Nashville were some of the best years of our marriage. Our fifth son Mark was born in Nashville. If I had known we were going to have a string of boys I would have begun naming them Matthew, Mark, Luke, and John, representing the names of the first books in the New Testament. Mark is probably glad I did not adopted that policy because a fifth boy named "Acts" would have had a hard time of it.

We bought a home in one of the newer housing developments west of the city. We had purchased an older home when we lived in Nashville the first time, and to our dismay we later discovered that there was a racial detail in the deed's contract. We were told that the house could not be sold to a black person. We were appalled.

When we returned to Nashville we told the real estate agent that we would not buy a property that had a racial stipulation in the deed. Our new neighbors were Jewish, and we were surprised to find so many other Jewish families in our development. We later realized that racial stipulations also prevented Jews from buying homes with racial covenants in the deed. Since our new development did not have such a stipulation, Jewish families often purchased homes there. It was the early 1960s, and while these parts of the deeds might not have held up in court, they were an indication of the types of people that would not be welcome in a neighborhood. We were glad we avoided such areas and enjoyed the opportunity to get to know our new neighbors. We were invited to our first "bris", the Jewish circumcision ceremony and naming rite for a newborn boy.

My work in Nashville as the overseas personnel director was challenging and exciting. The task included the recruitment and orientation of ministers, educators, physicians, agriculturalists and others for overseas service. My office also was responsible for developing and managing personnel policies and overseeing the health and care of over five hundred missionaries and their children. This part of my job required me to travel to Africa, Asia, South America, and Central America.

Daily Bible reading had been a part of my early morning routine for years. During this period in Nashville I became more spiritually disciplined by adding time for reflection and for recognizing the presence of God. This period of spiritual growth was aided by working with men and women of deep faith and commitment. Traveling around the world and seeing the difference the Christian faith made also impressed me and made me want to better know and understand my God.

Although the work strained my mental and physical capacities, it became a new spiritual adventure. For the past three or four years when my physical disabilities were at their peak, I didn't have much energy for anything—including my relationships with my family or God. This was a now a time for new beginning for me, and I tackled it with relish.

With five children our lives were busy with school, Boy Scouts, athletics, jobs, and church. One summer one of our teenagers worked late nights at a restaurant and returned home well after midnight. Another son had a job that required him to leave home in the early hours of the morning for newspapers deliveries. There were nights when the lights in our house were never turned off, and an observant neighbor quipped, "The sun never sets in the Coffin's house."

Lou Alice and I began to notice that we seldom had time for each other. She suggested that we begin our day an hour earlier at five o'clock in the morning and spend that hour together before the busy day began. I thought it was a great idea. Those moments together had a profoundly positive effect on our marriage. We had time to become friends again and to be thankful each day to live in God's world.

One of the rules in our family was that everyone had to be at breakfast when we ate at seven. It did not matter what time a person went to bed or what time that person arose for the day. Family members were required to come together for breakfast and a morning prayer. In spite of the frequent grumbling it did help build our family life.

Lou Alice developed a unique ceremony when we had small children. When one of them had a particularly difficult day and needed cheering up she planned a special event. On those occasions the dejected child was placed on top of the refrigerator near our dining table. I believe that he was also given a crown to wear as he proudly looked down on us. There was something special about being able to eat on top of the world—or at least on top of the refrigerator.

Lou Alice and I also put some effort into developing our boys' faith. Sunday after Sunday, overcoming all of their protests and their sick claims, we would get them dressed and take them to Sunday school and church. We discovered that one of our sons was wearing his play clothes to church under his Sunday clothes. That way he could take off his good clothes on the drive home and be ready for play when we arrived there.

One year when the older boys were young teens I gave

them an advanced course in Christian education by taking them to visit some other churches. We went in the summer when the preacher at our home church was on vacation. Attendance is usually down on those Sundays because many people believe that God isn't checking the roll if the preacher is away on vacation.

We first visited a Methodist church, and the boys found that the service was similar to our Presbyterian worship. However, there was more emphasis on living a holy life in that form of worship. This was not surprising since the Methodists came from Charles Wesley's emphasis on the importance of disciplined living. I reminded the boys that Wesley developed some rules or methods for holy living, and that these methods gave that church the name "Methodist."

When we visited the Baptist church the boys were impressed with the indoor swimming pool at the front of the sanctuary. The baptismal pool reminded us that the Baptists tend to emphasize the importance of the conversion experience and of baptism by immersion—giving them the name "Baptist."

Our visit to the Catholic Church reminded us that this group sees itself as the universal church. The word, catholic, is sometimes used as a synonym for universal or worldwide. On our way home from that worship service we discussed the important place the rituals of the mass and confession play in the life of practicing Catholics.

As a part of the church history lesson, I explained to the boys that the name "Presbyterian" grew out of the Reformation reaction to the idea that one man, the Pope alone, could speak for God. In response to that concept John Calvin designed a more democratic church governed by elders or "presbyters," as the New Testament named those who were called to govern the church. We Presbyterians derive our name from those early presbyters.

Our last lesson in church history was our most impressive. We visited a Pentecostal church on the north side of Nashville. The church was named the Evangel Temple and a man named Jimmy Snow was the preacher. He was the son of the country music singer Hank Snow. Jimmy's wife, Carol, played the electric organ surrounded by a group with guitars and a drum. Carol was also the child of country music stars Lulu Belle and Scotty. Remember, we lived in Nashville, Tennessee and country music was in the blood of the city.

I led the way into the sanctuary that Sunday, and the three boys followed me into a pew on the side towards the back. It was a wonderful service. The music was very lively. During the pastoral prayer the whole congregation joined in with their own words and strange sounds all at the same time. The sermon was enthusiastic and was followed by an alter call and invitation with these words, "Every head bowed, every eye closed, all those who want to give their lives to Jesus will show it by coming down front. This may be your last chance. You may have an automobile crash on the way home and be killed and spend eternity in the fires of hell if you do not come forward."

My head was bowed when my son John, sitting next to me, poked me in the ribs and said, "Sam has gone down front, and we can't let him go by himself." I looked up to see Sam walking down the aisle almost to the front of the sanctuary, followed by his brother Paul, a few steps behind him and John leaving our pew. What's a father to do? I followed them down front.

We were led out of the sanctuary by a group of men who took us down the hall to a room where they had us kneel. Two or three men hovered over each of us and began mumbling words unintelligible to us. It dawned on me that they were speaking in tongues, and wanted us to do the same. I knew about speaking in tongues, but did not have the gift of glossallia. These strange words sounded very much like one of the African languages we had learned, so I said these few words in Tshiluba, "Tshilamba etshi tshidi tshimpe. Bilamba ebi bidi bimpe." That seemed to satisfy the men escorting us. The boys, who had also been in Africa, mimicked my African words, and we had passed the test.

I felt relief a bit too early. The congregation was still in the sanctuary singing what must have been the fifteenth verse of "Just As I Am." They were waiting for us to return to demonstrate our newly acquired spiritual gifts. At that moment the "fires of hell" that the preacher had mentioned earlier sounded like a more acceptable option to me.

As we marched back down the hall towards the sanctuary there was a fire door leading outside. My feet took me out that door and the boys followed. My dreams of a quiet escape ended when the door activated a very loud fire alarm and the congregation spilled out the front door of the sanctuary. We found our car and drove home in silence.

It was a sobering experience for us to be with these folks whose emphasis on the arrival of the Holy Spirit on the day of Pentecost had earned their church the name Pentecostal. While most Presbyterian worship services certainly lacked the vitality of a Pentecostal service we were glad to return to our familiar surroundings.

The experiences of these churches with different histories and what they held most important reminded me that while we have our differences, we need each other. The discipline of the Methodists, the importance of conversion and baptism for the

Baptists, the historical and universal outlook of the Catholics, the enthusiasm of the Pentecostals, the sense of order of the Presbyterians and the traditions of other branches of Christ's Church are important gifts. We need to accept and learn from each other. Criticism and rejection should come from God and not from us.

During this time of my work in Nashville, I met and became friends with Sam and Helen Walton from Arkansas who were to become the founders of the Wal-Mart Corporation. I had traveled to Little Rock to make a presentation to a group of Presbyterians in a hotel. After the presentation I came out to the lobby to meet another friend for dinner. My friend Joe Norton, a Little Rock physician, was visiting with Sam Walton when I arrived. They had met before and Sam was there to pick up Helen who was in the meeting.

Joe invited Sam and Helen to have dinner with us, and we ate in the dining room there. During the conversation Sam begin to describe his plans to start a number of general-purpose stores in small towns across the county. I was fascinated. I had just finished a demographic study of population shifts in this country and how that might influence the life of congregations. I was young and bursting with knowledge. Wanting to save Sam Walton from making a major business mistake, I explained to him that his plan would not work. The demographic shifts were going in the opposite direction, and people at that time were moving away from the small towns into the cities. Starting stores in small towns would be a drastic mistake. In addition, general all-purpose stores were too cluttered and difficult to keep stocked.

Sam also told us that they were going to call the stores Wal-Mart as an abbreviation for Walton's Markets. Full of vigor and youthful wisdom, I explained to him what a bad idea that would be. The name was too cutesy and did not sound dependable. People, at least in that day, wanted solid reliable family names like J. C. Penny or Sears and Roebuck. He needed to rethink the concept, location, and names for his stores if he was to be successful. He was attentive and courteous and paid for our dinner. Happily he did not heed my suggestions.

In later years I saw Sam and Helen occasionally, and they never mentioned my bad advice. One year, in Philadelphia at the annual denominational meeting of the Presbyterian Church, I was assigned a seat next to Helen. She was representing the Presbyterian Foundation. Those of us who were delegates were transported by bus from downtown hotels to the coliseum where we were meeting. One morning Helen realized that she had gotten off and left her purse on the bus. Lou Alice was standing nearby and offered to go look for it, but Helen decided to go herself. Lou Alice and I spent some time chuckling. Think about what a difficult time a thief would have trying to decide what to buy first. The possibilities were limitless with a credit card belonging to one who was at that time a member of the richest family in the world.

Nashville was a good place for us to raise our family. The 1960s ushered in a new day. Those were times of changes in our society that were both exciting and tragic. The civil rights movement brought hope for oppressed people but the violence surrounding the movement brought disgrace and shame. The assassinations of President John Kennedy, his brother Robert Kennedy and the great civil rights leader, the Reverend Martin Luther King, Jr., brought shock and sorrow to the nation.

Society accompanied by the civil rights movement was also making strides towards the equality of women. There were early signs of change in old institutions and new ways of thinking were taking roots. There were missteps, chaos, and abuses along the way, but it was clear that we were entering a new age.

One of the responsibilities of my job was to direct an orientation program for new missionaries that took place each summer at the Presbyterian retreat center in Montreat, North Carolina, in the beautiful Blue Ridge Mountains near Ashville. Each year about forty or fifty new missionaries and their children entered this two-month program. The classes included lessons in linguistics, the geography of their assigned countries, mission policy, and health precautions. The excitement and eagerness of the participants made this annual project one of the favorite parts of my job.

The first of June each summer our family would load up the station wagon and trailer with our five sons, the dog, the cat, the hamsters, the canary, our clothes, toys, athletic equipment, and everything else we would need for the summer. Then we would head for Montreat until the end of August. We had bought a big old boarding house with eight bedrooms in Montreat, and we spent the summer months there. The house became a home repair training school for our sons. We installed light fixtures and wall switches. We repaired pipes that had frozen and burst during the winter. We painted and wallpapered vast areas and conducted the constant routine maintenance required by an old house. The boys also made friends with other summer visitors, and enjoyed the freedom of wandering around the small retreat community.

Our house had a long front porch that looked out over the mountains. The rocking chairs on the porch were a favorite gathering spot for our family and for friends who would be in

Montreat for vacations or conferences. The house where Billy Graham and his family lived before they built their present home was just up the street from our house. Their large St. Bernard was a frequent visitor to our front porch.

The big Southern Baptist conference center, Ridgecrest, was a few miles from Montreat. Each summer many of the thousands of Baptists who came to Ridgecrest for conferences would drive to Montreat to see where the most famous Southern Baptist evangelist lived. They would stop Presbyterians by the side of the road and ask where Billy Graham lived. The standard Presbyterian answer was, "Billy who?" The Baptist would say, "Billy Graham." The appropriate Presbyterian response was, "I don't believe I have ever heard of him."

One afternoon five of my minister friends and I were sitting on our porch when the Graham's big Saint Bernard named Sampson, wandered up. The dog went from person to person to be petted and scratched. One of the preachers challenged the others to start his next sermon with a sentence that would begin with, "This past week as I was looking out over the Smokey Mountains and patting Billy Graham's dog, I thought..." The words that followed were to weave into the sermon.

I gave each of them a postcard that they were to mail back to me with a report on how they finished the sentence. The responses were not very imaginative. Words like, "As I was patting Billy Graham's dog last week, I remembered a dog I had as a child and how faithful he was to me," followed by a lesson on being faithful. Or, "As I was patting Sampson, Billy Graham's dog, and looking out at the Smokey Mountains, I was overwhelmed by the power and beauty of God's creation." All of the preachers reported that while many in the congregation may not have remembered all that was said in the sermon, most members did ask why their minister had been patting the well-known evangelist's dog. At least for a while the preacher had the congregation's attention.

After the first week of August each year the training program I directed would be completed and I would take some vacation time. It was then that the boys and I went to Sunset Beach, a small island on the Atlantic Ocean near the northern border of South Carolina. Keeping up with the five boys at the beach would not have been a vacation for Lou Alice so she stayed in Montreat for her only real vacation from her duties as a mother.

We planned our beach trip each year to meet my two friends Bill and Harry and their families. The five adults and ten children ate, fished, crabbed, swam, hiked, and played together with enthusiasm. One of our favorite games was crab roulette. We would form a large circle holding hands on the beach. We were all barefooted and would release a number of large crabs in the middle of the circle. If a crab was headed for your bare feet as it raced to escape, the temptation, of course, was to move away. The losers were those who broke the circle.

A tradition was begun of trying to hide one of the crab baits, usually an old chicken neck, in another's car on the last night of vacation before the trip home. The baits produced an unforgettable odor after they had been in the sun for several days. Under floor mats, behind dashboards, under the hood, or even in a hubcap were favorite hiding places. The competition became so stiff that it was necessary to post guards by the cars the night before our morning departure. We all had a long day's drive home and we finally decided that for the sake of safety we needed to stop the game. The substitute became a contest with a wooden carving of an African man's head about five inches high. The goal was to place the object among the belongings of one of the families so that they wouldn't find it until they returned home. Laundry bags, sacks of sugar, or in the bottom of an ice chest were favorite hiding places. Each year the prize would be moved to another family.

When our children grew up we stopped taking those beach vacations together but the African man tradition continued. We all lived in different parts of the country, yet we found ways to deliver the prize. When my friend Harry was teaching at Yale, we called the cleaners where he sent his clothes in New Haven, and asked them to place the head in his laundry so that Harry found it when he opened his box of fresh shirts. His brother Bill was the minister in Charlottesville, Virginia, and one Sunday as Bill began the morning worship the African head was looking up at him from the pulpit. For several years there was no activity with the head, and I assumed that it had been lost. It was hard to know though since part of the tradition was that no one ever mentioned that it had been passed to him and was in his possession.

Some years later I was being given a Doctor of Divinity from Austin College. I wasn't eager for the honor and at first declined, but I finally relented. Lou Alice was also a graduate of the college and we had not been back to the school in years. It was a fun weekend for us. We had met at the school over forty years earlier, and we were having a good time with our memories.

Lou Alice was disappointed that she could not find her name on a low wall on the campus that listed all of the former graduates. Someone had to point out to her that she was looking for her name in the wrong place. She had forgotten that her maiden name was West and was looking in the section with names beginning with a "C" for Coffin. It was a good sign that our marriage was going to hold.

During the graduation ceremony I was sitting on the platform in my special robe when we finally came to the awarding of degrees. I was called to stand for them to place the Doctor of Divinity hood over my shoulders. Then a citation was read from a folder exaggerating my accomplishments. There was a long paragraph about my service in Africa and my sponsorship of African art. I should have seen it coming. Attached to the folder was our little pal the wooden African head. Did I mention that my friend Harry was President of the College and that another good friend was the on the Board of the Trustees?

The last time I saw the wooden head was when I put it on the top shelf of a kitchen cabinet in the house where Harry and his wife lived in Arizona. I always assumed that the winner of this game would be the one who put the prize in the casket of one of the other three of us. Harry died and gave his body for medical use so I had no chance of winning that time. I've begun to understand that the head will live on long after we are gone.

My job in Nashville included both overseas and domestic travel. One of my assignments was to visit the students at seminaries to challenge them with the opportunity for overseas missionary service. I always looked forward to visiting the seminary in Austin where we had lived and still had friends.

I usually planned that trip at the time that the seminary there held a special lecture series. That let me visit with friends from around the state who had come for the event. One year on the flight to Austin I found myself sitting by a man I had known when I was a pastor there. Ken had been the rector of an Episcopal church nearby and we had become friends. As we visited on the trip I came up with a way to surprise my friends who were meeting my flight.

The lecture series that year at the Seminary was to be given by Dr. Robert McAfee Brown, a distinguished theologian who had attended the Vatican Council in Rome as an Official Protestant Observer. That council meeting was to bring about significant changes in the Catholic Church, and Professor Brown was to offer us his impressions.

My Episcopal rector friend, Ken, had on his clerical collar and black suit and looked very ecclesiastical. I suggested that when we arrived in Austin and found the persons who were meeting me, I would introduce him as a Catholic Bishop who had been sent as the Official Catholic Observer. We would explain that he had been sent to Austin to hear the Protestant Observer's report on the Vatican Council. He was a good sport and agreed to go along with the hoax.

When we arrived, one of my friends, Walter, who was then a professor at the seminary, met us first. I decided to let him in on the fraud. The other person who had come to meet me was my friend Bill, who was a pastor in Lubbock at that time. Bill was something of a scholar and prided himself on keeping up with the recent meeting in Rome. When we introduced him to this Bishop who had come as the Catholic Observer to watch the report of the Protestant Observer of the Vatican Council, he was thrilled.

Walter offered to give Ken a ride to his hotel downtown and, as the fake Catholic Observer, he sat in the front seat. Bill began to lean forward from the backseat and ply the would-be Bishop with heavy questions about obscure parts of the report from the Vatican Council. Walter interrupted the theological questions with other questions like, "Tell us the truth, Father. Do you priests really only eat fish on Friday or do you sometimes slip in a hamburger?" (Do you remember the days when Catholics were not allowed to eat meat on Fridays?)

Then Walter would follow with an even cruder question. "And what about those nuns? Is there sometimes a little hanky panky going on with you priests?" During this inappropriate questioning, Bill was scandalized. After we let the imposter Vatican Observer out at his hotel Bill let Walter have it with some righteous indignation for his indecent behavior.

Later that evening with a group of friends at Walter's house, Bill described with great annoyance Walter's crude behavior in front of the Catholic guest. He pointed out that the Catholic Observer must have been very insulted because he had not even come to hear Dr. Brown's lecture that evening. It was then that we let Bill in the hoax and laughed about his wasted indignation.

A quick follow up. The next year I was flying into Austin to be met again by Walter and Bill. On the flight I noticed that a man sitting across the aisle from me looked familiar. I thought that I remembered him from a meeting at a church in Beaumont. After some hesitation I finally spoke to him, introduced myself, and asked if we had not met earlier. He said that he did not think so but was glad to meet me. He said that his name was Thurgood Marshall. At that moment and with great embarrassment I knew why he looked familiar. His face was on the cover of Time magazine that week. He had just been nominated by Lyndon Johnson, the United States President, to serve as the Attorney General and was later to become a Supreme Court Justice.

He was a good sport about my not recognizing him and we had an engaging conversation. He was going to Austin to speak and to be honored at Huston-Tillotson College, a United Methodist college in Austin. I told him about my hoax on that last trip to Austin and he enjoyed hearing about it. At that moment, I came up with a new idea since I was going to be met again by my friends Walter and Bill.

I could get off of the plane with my distinguished looking friend. They would immediately recognize him as the now famous Thurgood Marshall. To complete the prank I would introduce him to them as Roger Jones, an old friend from my hometown of Itasca. They would then have to be puzzled at how much he resembled the nominee for the office of Attorney General of the United States. I would revel in last year passing off a phony as the real thing and this year having the genuine article and claiming him to be someone else.

Unfortunately before I could complete the transaction a delegation from the college, including a band, arrived and prevented my introductions. As Dr. Marshall was introduced by the college hosts to the waiting crowd as the dignitary he really was, he looked over at us and gave us a smile and a nod of his head.

After our ten years in Nashville a reorganization of the structure of the denominational offices of the Presbyterian Church moved all of the national church offices to Atlanta, Georgia—including the overseas mission board function where I worked. We had enjoyed our time in Tennessee, had seen our children grow up and sent two off to college. But moving was not a new adventure for us, so we packed up for Atlanta.

While we lived in Atlanta, Lou Alice's mother, Syd, became ill. My mother-in-law lived in Dallas, and after her husband died she had moved into a retirement home. Her health was not good, and we all decided that it would be helpful for her to be closer to us. She agreed to come live in a retirement facility in Atlanta.

One of my assignments each Sunday was to go to Syd's apartment and play dominoes with her. She kept score during our Sunday games and announced one day that, by her count, I then owed her twenty-two thousand dollars. I was not surprised because we had probably played twenty two thousand games. I did not worry too much about the debt because Lou Alice was the only heir to her estate where the debt would finally be lodged.

Each Sunday after our domino game my mother-in-law and I would attend a worship service for the residents in the retirement home. A number of churches in Atlanta had agreed to provide the worship, and each church was responsible for one service each quarter. The arrangement was good except that three months is a long time for a congregation to remember an assignment. Occasioinally a leader would forget, and no one would come to lead the worship. The residents would be disappointed when this happened so one Sunday I agreed to be the substitute. After that anytime a church neglected to send a worship leader, I would be pressed into service.

I had a simple system for leading the service unprepared. I would let the residents choose the hymns we would sing. My voice does not lend itself to being a song leader, but I would take comfort in a story my friend Jim once told me. His singing voice was a vigorous low monotone, and he used it loudly. His wife, his friends, and finally his minister suggested that he not sing the hymns so loudly in church. His response was, "I have talked to God about this and we have an arrangement. If I keep my financial pledge to the church paid up to date I can sing as loudly as I want." So I led the singing in the retirement home with great vigor, because someone needed to do it and my church pledge was usually paid up.

After the singing I would ask for prayer requests and lead the congregation in a pastoral prayer. Next I would ask for a Scripture passage that someone would like to hear. After reading the designated passage from the Bible, I would preach on that text. Preaching on a surprise text was not as difficult as it might seem. Ordinarily the requested Scripture passage would be a familiar one such as the twenty third Psalm, "The Lord is my Shepherd," or John 3:16, "God so loved the world." These readings would be familiar passages that most preachers have used before, and it was not difficult for me to give a brief devotional that coordinated with the text.

I was put to the test one Sunday when an old man requested an obscure Old Testament passage about dogs eating children and old people. I bluffed through it without batting an eye. After the service he came up and complained, "You didn't play fair. You just preached your usual sermon about how much God loves and cares for us." I did not worry about his criticism, because I thought that my lesson was an appropriate message for most sermons—especially for lonely folks in a retirement home who do not need to spend their time thinking about being eaten by dogs.

For most of our time in Atlanta Lou Alice and I attended a church near downtown in an area that had once been a very affluent part of the city. As times changed the city had spread out and some parts of the area around the church had become rather rundown and neglected. The congregation was composed of some members from the earlier wealthy neighborhood and other members from the now much less affluent area. It was a wonderful mixture.

Two incidents from our time there have stuck in my mind. One Sunday as the organist was playing the prelude, an older woman in very shabby clothes came in and went to a pew near the front of the sanctuary. After she had been seated for a few moments she began to cry. Her weeping moved on to heavy sobs of grief. It was an awkward moment. Most of us were not sure what to do.

A middle-aged man sitting a few rows behind her stood up and walked to where she was sitting. He then sat down next to her, put his arm around this stranger, and held her while she sobbed. He did not seem to mind that his expensive suite was rubbing against her filthy clothes. The man was a wealthy physician from a leading family in the city. Throughout the service he continued to sit close to her and give her comfort. I later learned that after the service he followed through with arrangements for her to have decent housing, medical care, and other needed aid.

This came during a period when I was having some questions about churches and how effective they really were in demonstrating God's love in the world. I was even questioning if I was supposed to spend my life as a part of this institution. However, seeing the man holding that sad woman and later knowing that he made arrangements for a better life for her left a strong impression on me. The scene reminded me that the church's role is to put its arms around the hurts and pain of the world. I had a glimpse of God at work that morning as I watched the man put his arms around the sobbing woman.

That congregation gave me another good lesson in how God works. One Sunday there was to be an infant baptism for the baby of a young couple who had recently come to the United States from a country in South America. Some members of the church had helped them find housing and jobs. Others had helped them work on their immigration process. Growing out of these friendships the young couple became members of the church, and not long afterward a child was born to them.

In the Presbyterian tradition of infant baptism, when the baby was a few weeks old, the baptism was scheduled for an eleven o'clock worship service. During the service when the time came for the baptism, the couple was called to come to the front of the sanctuary. As the couple from South America came forward that Sunday, the minister and the congregation could see that they did not have the baby with them. There was a whispered huddle with the couple and the minister near the baptismal font. Following this conference the minister told the congregation that there had been a misunderstanding when the couple was preparing for the baptism. They had not understood that they were to bring the baby with them.

The minister calmly explained to the congregation that there would be a slight delay in the service. The couple was returning to their apartment a few blocks from the church to retrieve the baby who was being cared for by a neighbor that morning. During the recess church members visited with each other until the young couple returned with the infant and the baptism took place. That incident sticks in my mind. It reminds me that while the church tries to demonstrate God's love and be a sign of the Kingdom of Heaven in this world, we are frequently as awkward and clumsy as a newborn calf in our efforts. In spite of our mistakes God uses us.

While we lived in Atlanta a significant event for Presbyterians took place. Over a century earlier, as the nation had become divided between the North and the South by the Civil War the church had also divided into two denominations—a northern Presbyterian church and a southern Presbyterian church. Finally, in 1983, the decision was made to reunite these two separated denominations. The northern branch had its denominational offices in New York and the southern offices were in Atlanta. Following the reunion it was decided to locate the new Presbyterian offices at a neutral site. That site was to be Louisville, Kentucky.

In this organization I was asked to be the director of the office of communication and stewardship so we said good-bye to Atlanta and greeted our new life in Kentucky. It was new in more ways than geographically. For almost thirty years children had been in our home. Now the last of five sons had departed and Lou Alice and I were alone again. We were starting over again in a new place with just the two of us.

NORTH TO LOUISVILLE

My job in Louisville required frequent air travel. While the new headquarters building was being prepared that first year, part of my division's staff of sixty was still in Atlanta, part in New York, and a small part was with me in Louisville. It was not an unusual workweek for me to spend two days in Atlanta, two days in New York, and one day in Louisville. After the staff was assembled in Louisville, continued travel was necessary to make new contacts across the country, and to begin the process of pulling the two parts of the church together. The airlines became a second home for me.

Louisville was a friendly place to live. It was a nice mixture of the North and the South. We were reminded that it was part northern in the winter of 1994. The temperature dropped to twenty-two degrees below zero, and there were eighteen inches of snow on the ground. Many homes lost electricity and had no heat for several days. This happened to friends of ours, and to their dismay all their houseplants froze. After they used their store of firewood, they started burning pieces of furniture in the fireplace to provide some heat. We, and our houseplants, were much more fortunate. In our area of town the power stayed on.

The first Saturday in May is a special day for Louisville because that is the day of the Kentucky Derby. The celebration begins several weeks earlier and culminates with the horse races on Saturday afternoon. Celebrities from around the world gather in the crowd of over one hundred thousand fans.

Tickets for good seats at the races are expensive and difficult to obtain. The infield inside the oval racing track is made available at a reduced price, and it becomes the venue for the younger party crowd. Imbibing mint juleps during the afternoon enhances the celebration for many. It is almost impossible to see the racetrack from the infield, but it is a great party place. One year I went to the infield for the Derby, and while wandering around I found one of the few places a person could see the finish line. A man who spent his time going to major sporting events had staked out that spot. At each event he would secure a place where the television camera was certain to scan his presence. At the crucial moment when the camera focused on his location, he would display a large sign with the inscription, "John 3:16." This was his attempt to remind the television audience of millions that, "God so loved the world," the words from the Biblical reference on his sign. The man with the sign was jealously guarding the little area near the finish line where the camera would televise him and his sign at the exciting end of the race. I talked to him about his plan, and he confessed that he was worried. His partner, who was to hold the other end of the large sign, had not appeared. Naturally I volunteered to substitute. He accepted my offer and I was one of the few people in the infield in a location to see the finish of the Kentucky Derby that year. I also had an opportunity to proudly smile at the millions of people watching on television as I held up one end of the John 3:16 sign.

One day I looked at the calendar, and was surprised to find that my sixty-fifth birthday had arrived, and that a retirement party was planned for me. The day after that party I joined the staff of one of the largest churches in Louisville, the Harvey Browne Presbyterian Church. It was a great experience for me. Overnight I was transformed from one of those out of touch radical denominational church leaders into a friendly and lovable old pastor and with no effort on my part or change in my inner life. The experience gave me an opportunity to participate more fully in church members' daily joys and pain.

While I was on the staff, the church hired a new senior pastor. Soon after he arrived I went in for a visit with him. I first explained how glad I was that he had come to the church and that I believed he had the right gifts for the congregation. I went on to tell him that not long before, a pastor in a nearby church had been accused of sexual harassment by one of its members. The presbytery, the body responsible for the oversight of pastors in that area, held a long investigation. Interviews were held with the accused, the accuser, with other staff members, and with church members. The painful investigation process had taken weeks and had been an extremely difficult time for everyone. After explaining that situation to our new pastor, an attractive young man, I went on to explain that should he ever be accused of sexual harassment we would not have to worry about a long painful investigation by the presbytery. I did not think that would be helpful for him, his accuser, or the church. If such accusations were made I would immediately carry on my own investigation. If I found that the charges were true, there would be no complicated trial. I grew up in Texas and still owned my father's handgun and knew how to use it. If I found him guilty, I would immediately shoot him and end the disgraceful situation. At my age I would not even worry about the punishment for my crime.

Some years later he and I were in a sexual harassment workshop required of all Presbyterian pastors in that area. During the meeting he told the group about the conversation I had with him when he first arrived. He concluded by saying, "And I believed him!" I might add that he has been in that church for over a decade and there have been no charges filed. We became and still are very close friends. He has been a wonderful companion.

One of my responsibilities for the church was making hospital calls. Having spent many days as a hospital patient, I understand that being away from home in an institutional setting when you are sick can be a disheartening experience. Even as a hospital visitor it was easy for me to feel intimidated with all of the doctors, nurses, and technicians racing around the hallways. I finally bought a stethoscope and hung it around my neck as I made hospital calls. It was surprising how much more secure I felt, and how much more respect the hospital staff gave me when I was wearing that simple devise. I did not listen to any heartbeats with it, but I did try to comfort some troubled hearts.

One of the hospitals had a unique respect for ministers. The hospital had a prime parking location labeled, "Reserved for Clergy Only." There was another parking lot reserved for doctors, but it was further from the hospital than the clergy lot. One day as I was parking in the clergy lot, a man pulled his car into the space next to mine. As he got out of his car I noticed that he was wearing a white medical jacket and had a stethoscope around his neck. I could not resist calling out to him as I pointed to the "Clergy Only" sign, "You forgot your Bible!" He looked at the sign, frowned at me, and muttered something that I do not think was very religious. He returned to his automobile and roared off toward the doctors' lot. A few weeks later there was a change in the location for clergy parking. It was further from the hospital's entrance and the lot for doctors had been moved closer. I began to regret my misguided humor with the doctor and wondered if I had killed the goose that laid the golden egg.

Another event from my hospital calls stands out in my mind. One Saturday evening I received a telephone call that some members of our church had been involved in an automobile accident. They had been taken to the hospital emergency room. Lou Alice and I went down to the University Hospital that provided care for the city's trauma cases. We found the members of our congregation who had been returning home from participating in a hand bell concert in a neighboring town.

If you have ever been in a hospital's emergency room for trauma victims on a Saturday night, you know that it is a place of bedlam, and that you are going to be in for a long wait. Two of the church members had been seriously injured and were being examined. This was not a quick process. They required X-rays and other tests. One of the church members had head injuries and was admitted to the hospital. The other one was finally discharged, and a family member came to take her home.

We spent several hours in the waiting room that Saturday evening. It was a good place for people watching. People of all ages and backgrounds were coming in for treatment. It was a mesh of rich and poor people. Most of the people were worried and distraught. But what made the evening really interesting was watching as they tried to leave the emergency room.

As people tried to leave they would find that the exit door

wouldn't open when pushed. They would look around and see a sign next to the door that said:

TO OPEN DOOR
HOLD HAND OVER EYE

It was fun to watch as someone read that sign and then after looking around sheepishly put a hand over one of his or her eyes and pushed the door. The door still would not open. Everyone in the waiting room took a turn at going over and pointing to the wall near the door. There on the wall was a pad with an electric eye on it. When a hand was held over the electric eye the door would automatically open. It was a good lesson for me that simple instructions are not always the best answers. Those few often-misunderstood words on the sign about how to open the emergency room's exit door became a good reminder for me as a person giving spiritual advice. Using too few words or offering advice that is too simple may lead someone to foolish actions.

After several years of visiting patients in the hospital, the tables turned and I became a patient. I'd had some earlier signs of heart trouble that had been diagnosed as a silent heart attack so I went to the hospital for a routine heart exam. Before the day was over I was taken to the operating room to experience the marvel of open-heart surgery. In this process my blood circulatory system was connected to a machine that pumped the blood and added oxygen to it. Then the surgeons could deflate my lungs, get them out of the way and stop my heart from beating. Once my heart was stopped they performed quintuple bypass surgery. As my heartbeat was stopped for this seven-hour operation that went into the evening hours, Lou Alice was left alone in the waiting room after everyone else had departed. She says she thinks that her heart stopped too.

The surgery was a traumatic experience for me. It was not only a physically trying experience. It was also a kind of spiritual crisis. Through the years I have developed a spiritual routine that includes morning prayers, daily morning Bible reading and evening prayers. I also set some traps for myself throughout the day. At several different times I remember that I belong to God and that God is watching over me. But following that surgery God's presence in my life seemed to me to have disappeared. It was not that I lost my faith. It was just that it seemed that God had gone away and my prayers did not seem to go anywhere. Lou Alice brought my devotional material to the hospital and read it to me, but God still seemed absent. I resented the fact that God was not there when I most needed the presence of the Holy Spirit.

But then things changed for me. My wife stood by my bed and held my hand. One of my sons received word of my surgery as he was going to his car leaving work that afternoon. Without going home to pack he immediately began to drive the 400 miles from his parking lot to the hospital in Louisville where I was. Another son in South Florida received word of my surgery and went to the airport to catch the first plane to come to see me. Our other sons came. The pastors of our church and friends begin to arrive and to send cards and to telephone. And then it dawned on me. These family members and friends were signs of God's love and presence in my life. My health had taken me out of the game, and I was on the bench unable to play. But the love of my family and friends were God's expressions of love for me. This was the church at work.

My recovery from the heart surgery was delayed by an extended bout with pneumonia. The long process of recuperation slowed down life for us and gave us an opportunity to think about the future. We decided that we were at a time when we would like to be geographically closer to our sons, daughters-in-law, and grandchildren. We began to plan our twenty-fourth move. Lou Alice has sometimes commented that it is easier to move than it is to clean the house.

THE VILLAGE

Our new home is in Presbyterian Village, a retirement community near Atlanta, Georgia. Two of our sons and their families live within an hour's drive and the other three sons are in the adjacent states of Florida and Tennessee. We now live in a delightful, small home on the side of a hill looking down over the sixty-acre wooded campus with a lake in the center. In addition to houses and duplexes there is a large apartment building, an assisted living facility, a nursing home, and a dementia center. A wide variety of activities, events, trips and programs are available for the residents. A large hospital is on the property next to the campus. Almost three hundred folks live here, and it has the neighborly feel of a small town. When we moved in neighbors came to our door with words of welcome and gifts of food. We think that our moving days are over. So now in 2007, sixty-one years after Lou Alice and I had our first date, we believe that we are located here for life. It is not a bad feeling after all of our moves.

Our lives are still busy with a daily exercise class and other activities. We also spend a significant amount of time in most older adults' favorite pastime—going to doctors' appointments. Our doctors provide wonderful medical care, and we like the slower pace of retirement that provides more space for reflection.

The influence of my immediate family and their significant role in my life has become clearer to me. I've often mentioned

Lou Alice. However, my words are totally inadequate to express what I feel for her. I cannot imagine my life without her, nor could I overemphasize how important she is and has been to me. I have sometimes remarked to her in jest, "We have had fifty happy years of marriage. Not bad for having been married fifty-seven years." We've actually been in love for over sixty years. There have been some struggles for us, usually when one of us has tried to change the other, but neither of us ever seriously considered cutting the other one loose. It occurred to me early in our marriage that Lou Alice liked me more than she liked her mother. I was never worried about her going home. As double insurance against that possibility I took her to Africa so that she could not go home.

She has been a great wife and mother. I have learned some important lessons from her character. She not only works long and hard, but she insists on doing things right and properly. My nature has always been to just get everything done as quickly as possible and with the least amount of effort. I need a daily example that there is a better way than my own haphazard style.

I also tend to think of Lou Alice as spirituality with hands and feet. I have some training in spiritual matters. I have a graduate theological degree. I would never consider making a grocery list or a "to do" list during a worship service. Yes, she has! Daily Bible reading does not seem to be a requirement for her life as it is for mine. People who act religious are not her role models.

Having said that about her, I admit that I do not know anyone who spends more time thinking about and meeting the needs of other people—family, friends, and strangers. These acts may not be grandiose or public, but a day seldom goes by that she does not think about someone and do something to help him or her. She is an active model of the great commandment to love God and neighbor. For me, that is spirituality with hands and feet, and I have learned so much from her.

I have mentioned the birth of each of our five sons but have not dwelt much on their lives. They are the pride of my life. I want to relate some stories about them but I will not mention their names to protect the accused. Sometimes I think that one of a child's main jobs is to embarrass parents and to keep mom and dad humble. For instance I still meet old friends around the country who like to remind me of the night they were at our home for a party. Sometime during the evening the telephone rang. It was a call from the police station. One of the boys had been arrested for disturbing the peace, and he would remain in jail until the $120 bond was paid in cash. I did not want him to spend the night in jail, but I didn't have that much cash, and this was in the days before ATMs. We stopped the party, and I passed a collection hat among our guests. When I delivered the required $120, the son was released from jail.

Here was his story. He said he had gone to a house to collect money from a customer on his paper route. The customer's bill was three weeks overdue, and the woman who came to the door said that she could not pay until her husband returned home from work later in the evening. The son waited nearby until he saw the husband arrive, and returned to the house to ring the doorbell again. No one came to the door. He rang again and there was no answer. As he continued ringing the bell the police arrived. The man in the house had called them to report a disturbance. This poor paper carrier was charged with disturbing the peace, hauled off and locked up. His time in jail was stressful for him, of course, and since he was instructed never to return to that house he was never able to collect from that family. The story was great entertainment for our guests that evening, and over the years whenever I see those friends they want to recall the evening they were asked to loan me money to free our teenager from jail.

We had another brush with the law one Sunday afternoon when our sixteen-year-old son was driving two fourteen-year-old girls home from putting up some sort of school display. On the way he accidentally ran a stoplight. Of course a patrolman was nearby, saw the violation, and pulled him over. The policeman was about to write a ticket when he noticed a can of beer on the floor of the car. So the three teenagers were taken to the juvenile detention center, and their parents were called.

I was sorry to be the first parent to arrive. That meant that the other parents gave me an earful of abusive language about their daughters being out with my son, and for being brought to the detention center for driving with alcohol in the car. Because the can of beer had not been opened, and because my son claimed that it did not belong to him but had been left in the car by someone else, the only charge was running a stoplight. He later blamed that whole affair on bad luck. He made the same plea when he and a young woman were caught in what was later called a "compromising position" in the church parlor. A group of women came in for a meeting and there the teenagers were. Having to face those women each Sunday when we attended worship was plenty of punishment.

One year I was in a jewelry store buying a birthday present for Lou Alice. I wrote a check for the gift and the woman who was waiting on me noticed my name. "Your name is Coffin, I noticed on your check," she said. "By your address I see that we live in the same neighborhood. Do you happen to have any children?" she asked. "Yes," I replied, and glad to meet a neighbor, told her the names of our five sons. Then with great displeasure she explained her interest. "A few weeks ago we had a concrete patio poured at the back of our house. When we went to bed that evening it was a beautiful clean surface. The next morning in a very prominent area in four-inch letters was the name of one of your sons—his first name, his middle name, and his last name. During the night while the cement was still wet he quite obviously came and wrote his name."

The son denied knowing anything about it, and thought that one of his friends must have done it for a joke. I wondered what friend would have known his middle name. In this case the bad luck was mine since I was the one who went to the jewelry store and wrote the check with my name and address on it.

We had another surprise one day when we received a letter from the principal of our local high school. The letter informed us that one of our sons had been permanently expelled for repeatedly breaking the rule forbidding smoking on the school grounds. I was pretty upset about it, but my son was not. In fact he was rather pleased to be kicked out because he really didn't like school and was glad to be finished with it. As a footnote I will add that he did finally graduate from high school and college and later earned a graduate degree. I'm happy also to report that, by his own choice, he doesn't smoke anymore.

On another afternoon there was a knock on our back door. It was the grandmother who was staying next door for a few days with the children while their parents were away on a trip. The grandmother asked me, her voice full of anxiety, "Is it alright if your cat is in our refrigerator?" It took a while for me to unravel the mystery. Our son had wandered into the house next door and our cat had followed him. It was a friendly neighborhood. Either hunger or curiosity had led our five-year-old to open the neighbor's refrigerator. The cat also interested in its contents must have walked up and sniffed inside. Most probably our son helped the cat up on a shelf and then closed the door. "No, it is not appropriate for our cat to be in your refrigerator and I will certainly have a consultation with our son about this," was my embarrassed response to her question.

When our three oldest sons were teenagers and had learned to drive I could not resist buying a huge old black Cadillac hearse that I saw on a used car lot. It only cost one hundred dollars. What could be more fun for a family named "Coffin?" As the hearse went by neighborhood kids would call out, "Here come the coffins!"

The good part was that through good times and tough times we have remained good friends. While I have told stories of embarrassing times, there were plenty of times we were very, very proud of those boys. As I lived and loved with them I leaned to appreciate the vitality and adventuresome spirit of youth. I have a sense of comfort and pride now that all of them are men of high integrity and moral standing.

Five Sons in Montreat—2000

Our lives have also been enriched with daughters-in law and grandchildren. I marvel at how out of the billions of people in the world each of our sons has found the exact person that would make his life whole. It was as if there was a powerful magnetic force that drew each set of two people together. Divine guidance perhaps? Our sons' wives have accepted Lou Alice and me into their lives and have let us share our lives with them in very special ways. And as you would expect, this grandfather believes that each of our five grandchildren is extraordinary. Their ages are spread over almost two-dozen years so we have participated with them in all of the pains and pleasures of life from infancy through adulthood. What a gift!

Our family is now geographically spread over three states, but we stay in touch with visits, e-mails, and telephone calls.

With the addition of daughters-in law and grandchildren there are now sixteen of us. They show that they care about us in many different ways. We meet each year for a reunion lasting for a week or a long weekend. We have gathered on the Florida beach, in the mountains of Tennessee and North Carolina, on the island of Nantucket, on a Caribbean cruse, at Yellowstone Park, and have made visits to England and Italy. While the settings have been fun and interesting, the relationships we renew on these trips have been even more significant. I have been blessed many ways in my life with good friends, interesting jobs, travel, and challenging work. But the most important gift of all has been the gift of family.

Family—Jackson Hole, Wyoming—2007

In retirement our more relaxed lifestyle has reminded me of the folly of my earlier days, but it has also helped me think more about my spiritual life. I am reminded of the line about old folks reading their Bibles more because they are cramming for the final exam. Actually, I may be reading my Bible less. For years I met my goal of reading four chapters a day in order to read through the Bible once each year. After sixty years of that regime I no longer require myself to follow that schedule. I do not necessarily spend less time with the Bible, but I do take more time to think about what I am reading and to look up passages in a commentary if I have questions about the meaning. In addition to my morning Bible reading I use a personal devotional meditation followed by the Presbyterian Mission Yearbook that focuses on a different part of the church in the world each day. Those three steps help me remember each morning the important triangle of God, my life and the world,

My evening prayers have taken on a variety of expressions. My earliest memories are of the ones I said when my mother put me to bed. I was taught the traditional, "Now I lay me down to sleep. I pray the Lord my soul to keep. If I should die before I wake, I pray the Lord my soul to take." Who ever thought it was a good idea to have a small child include the words, "If I should die before I wake..." in a petition as he was about to be left alone in a dark room?

To delay the moment of being left alone I often padded the "God bless" part of my prayers. The second paragraph of my prayer began with the words, "God bless Mother, Daddy, Sister Jane, Spot (the dog), Blackie (the cat), Aunt Janie, Uncle Sidney," followed by the names of my other aunts, uncles, cousins, friends, trees and plants in the yard, and anything else I could think of to stretch the prayer and delay my mother's departure.

Through the years my evening prayers have taken other forms. A few days before my wedding my mother made a suggestion to me. Since I was about to be married to this young woman from the East (east Texas, that is) perhaps it would improve my cultural standing if I started sleeping in pajamas. It was a new idea to me since I had thought that only small boys and old men slept in pajamas and that the rest of us slept in various forms of underwear. I was anxious to make my pending marriage work so I drove ten miles to a department store in Hillsboro, our county seat, and purchased two pair of pajamas. I had no experience in buying them and the ones I bought that day were a bit too snug. I did not put them on until I was married and immediately after the wedding we left Texas for Virginia. That meant that I couldn't return them and being frugal I wore those pajamas that were too tight for me for the next several years. Not only did I learn that it is important to buy the appropriate size pajamas, I learned that pajamas last forever. It takes years to wear out a pair. So I was tortured for a long time wearing my uncomfortably nightwear.

Then good fortune came my way when my Uncle Dan died. I suppose it wasn't such good fortune for him, it was a good turn for me. My uncle and his brother had established a very successful grocery business in Cleburne, Texas. After his death I inherited six pair of his pajamas. How rich would you have to be to own six pair of pajamas?

There was one small problem. My uncle was almost ten inches taller than I was. Lou Alice was able to hem up the sleeves and pants' legs so that I could find my hands and feet. But after a while another problem developed. The pajamas begin to wear out in a spot just above my ankles near the shins. Why pajamas would begin to show wear in such a strange place was a mystery to me. Then it dawned on me. My uncle was a religious man and when he wore the pajamas the worn place would have been at his knees. He had worn out the knees of his pajamas while kneeling in prayer beside his bed.

Kneeling for evening prayers was a solution to a problem for me. I had started saying my evening prayers after I got into bed at night and turned out the light. I would begin the prayer in earnest, but my mind would wander off to some other subject. I was constantly corralling my wandering mind back into the prayer. Sometimes I couldn't remember if I had finished the prayer, or if the prayer was still going on. I decided that if I were on my knees by the side of my bed I would be able to concentrate better, and probably my arthritis would tell me when it was time to stop. I found this practice of bedside nighttime prayers helpful.

Then another problem developed. I would I begin with a prayer of intersession for my own needs, and move on to a prayer for my family and friends. My mind would then widen out to pray for people in our country and in the world. As I finished and climbed into bed, my mind would still be filled with visions of starving children in Africa and abused people around the world. Those images haunted my thoughts as I tried to find sleep. It was not a good way to begin my rest.

I revised my plan. I would focus on intercessory prayer for the needs of the world, the country, my family and myself only in the morning. Evening prayers would focus on thoughts of thanks and adoration of God. It was a good idea, but I became increasingly aware of how inadequate my vocabulary for adoration and praise truly was. I was much better at telling God what needed to be done than I was at appreciating what God had done and was doing.

One Sunday in worship while singing a hymn, I realized what wonderful expressions of adoration the words of the hymn voiced. I then began to notice how many of the poems in hymns contained the words I needed for my evening prayers. So now I keep a hymnal by my bed. I know you are wondering but, no, I did not steal it from the church! It was given to me years ago and has my name engraved on the front. The poets who wrote those wonderful words of love, thanks, and adoration have provided me with the expressions I need each evening for my nightly prayers. Even if I had needed to steal the hymnal I believe that God and the church would have forgiven me because of how much it has enriched my evening prayers and given me the words I need to express my gratitude for life to my Creator.

A decal on the mirror of my car reads, "Objects in this mirror are closer than they appear." I think that means that the cars you see in that mirror are actually a lot closer than they look. The idea has repeatedly come to my mind as I reflect on my past. It has been over sixty years since I lived in Itasca, but those images still seem very close to me.

The clothesline of life has stretched a long way between my current life and those early days. In Itasca the incessant Texas winds constantly tossed the clothes as they dried on the clothesline in our backyard. Lou Alice and I have come and gone, here and there, moving twenty-four times as we have grown up, living in five different states. I have traveled in almost every state in this country and have lived in or visited Australia and countries in Europe, Africa, Asia, Central and South America. In spite of distance, travel, and time the basics of the life I learned in Itasca have been deeply imbedded in me. "Big I" may be closer than it appears.

My life today is in a very comfortable home with conveniences such as a washing machine and dryer, television, computer, and air conditioning. There is not a clothesline in sight. Stores that have food and articles from around the world surround us. There is no need to drive to the county seat to buy a pair of pajamas as was necessary when I bought my first pair.

But with all these wonderful physical changes the basics of life seem the same to me. My body has a lot more wear on it now than it did in "Big I," and it requires a lot more repair work, but it is still basically the same body. I have the same need for love and the need to be loved. I still have fears and joys, pain and pleasure, disappointments, and moments of satisfaction. I have traded the family of my early days—my father, mother, sister and brother-in-law—-for my wife, sons, daughters-in-law, and grandchildren. The sun still shines, and the moon and the stars are still in their orbits.

Lou Alice and I are at a wonderful time in our life together. About the only cloud on the horizon at this older stage is the probability that one of us at some future time will have to live without the other one. A few months ago I woke in the middle of the night with a pain in my chest. With my history of heart disease, I wondered if this was the heart attack that would take my life and separate me from Lou Alice. I then had an idea. I believed that I still had the strength to reach up and strangle her. That way we could leave this world together, and our major fear would be alleviated.

Then I began to have second thoughts. What if I did strangle Lou Alice and it turned out that my discomfort was caused by indigestion and was not a heart attack at all? What would I say when I called 911? "Hello, I thought that I was having a fatal heart attack and did not want to leave my wife behind so I strangled her." I chose not to put my misguided plan into action that night, and we continue to live happily together. I increasing admire God's plan that puts us together in families, and especially the gift that Lou Alice has been to me.

I recently learned that one of the landmarks in Itasca

has been removed. The structure we called "the standpipe" is gone. It was a water tower that provided pressure for our town's water supply. It was a round cylinder structure ten feet or so in diameter. The tower rose for what seemed like a mile into the sky, but it was probably more like two hundred or so feet. It was three times taller than any other structure in town and the huge light gray pipe extending into the sky could be seen in the countryside for miles around. On one side of the standpipe was a ladder of metal rod steps leading to the top. The rods began about ten feet above the ground to prevent easy access. That did not prevent young boys from temporarily borrowing a tall ladder from the volunteer fire department nearby and climbing to the top.

One afternoon on a dare I tried to climb to the top of that tower. I have always had a fear of heights, and that fear came into full play that afternoon. I do not know how high I actually climbed. It felt like I was ten miles up and the world was swaying around me below. I was frozen with fear. My hands were clinched around the metal rod, and I could not move up or down. In this paralyzed condition all sorts of thoughts went racing through my mind. Of course I prayed for help. God seemed to be off doing some other chore.

In that crisis I had a thought that has remained with me to this day. I knew that if somehow God could get me out of this, nothing would ever happen to me again in life that could be any more frightening. If I could only get past that panic situation, no other fear would ever be as great. I would always believe that any crisis could be somehow resolved. That has been mostly true. Since that time over half a century ago there have been moments when fear approached, but I would think of the time up on the standpipe when I was finally able to overcome my paralyzing fear and climb down. If I was able to do it that day, I knew I could do it again. This and other events from Itasca are the prism through which I view my life.

I learned:

> Courage and faith from the standpipe,
> About religion, sex and money from Six Ace,
> Faithfulness from friends,
> Love, honor, and respect from my family.
>   and
> from my life in Itasca and beyond,
> I gained an abiding assurance that
> in life and in death I belong to God
> who cares for me beyond my wildest
> dreams.

APPENDIX
CLOTHES LINE OF PLACES AND DATES

PLACES OF RESIDENCE

1929—1946 John, Itasca, Texas

1929—Lou Alice, Houston, Texas

1930—1946 Lou Alice, Beaumont, Texas

1946—1949—1950 Sherman, Texas

1949—1950—1952 Richmond, Virginia

1952—1953 Calvert, Texas

1953—Montreat, North Carolina

1953—1954 Brussels, Belgium

1954—1955 Luebo, Belgian Congo

1955—1957 Kinshasa, Belgian Congo

1957—Austin, Texas

1957—1960 Nashville, Tennessee

1960—1963 Austin, Texas

1963—1973 Nashville, Tennessee

1963—1975 Summers in Montreat, North Carolina

1973—1987 Atlanta, Georgia

1987—2005 Louisville, Kentucky

2005—Presbyterian Village, Austell, Georgia

DATES

1929   February 21—Birth of John M. Coffin IV, Hillsboro, Texas

1929   August 26—Birth of Lou Alice West, Houston, Texas

1946   May—John's High School Graduation, Itasca, Texas

1946   May—Lou Alice's High School Graduation, Beaumont, Texas

1949   May—John's Graduation from Austin College, Sherman, Texas

1950   May—Lou Alice's Graduation from Austin College

1951   August 31—Lou Alice and John's Wedding Beaumont, Texas,

1952   May—John's Graduation from Union Theological Seminary, Richmond, Virginia

1953   March 13—Birth of John M. Coffin V, Marlin Texas

1954   April 30—Birth of Paul Caswell Coffin, Brussels, Belgium

1956 January 11—Birth of Samuel West Coffin, Kinshasa, Belgium Congo

1960 June 1—Birth of David Laurence Coffin, Austin, Texas

1965 February 22—Birth of Mark McLean Coffin, Nashville, Tennessee

1996 February 28—John's Official Retirement, Louisville, Kentucky